Hebrews: A Guide

Hebrews: A Guide

ANDREW T. LINCOLN

T & T CLARK
A Continuum imprint
LONDON • NEW YORK

Published by T&T Clark

A Continuum imprint

The Tower Building, 11 York Road, London SE1 7NX
15 East 26th Street, Suite 1703, New York, NY10010

www.tandtclark.com

British Library Cataloguing-in-Publication Data
A catalogue record for this book is available from the British Library

ISBN 0567040321 (paperback)
ISBN 0567043630 (hardback)

Typeset by Servis Filmsetting Ltd, Manchester
Printed on acid-free paper in Great Britain by
MPG Books Ltd, Bodmin, Cornwall

Contents

Abbreviations

AB	*Anchor Bible*
ANTC	Abingdon New Testament Commentaries
BCE	Before the Common Era
BNTC	Black's New Testament Commentaries
CBQMS	Catholic Biblical Quarterly Monograph Series
CE	Common Era
CJT	*Canadian Journal of Theology*
ET	English translation
HTR	*Harvard Theological Review*
JBL	*Journal of Biblical Literature*
JSNTSup	*Journal for the Study of the New Testament*, Supplement Series
LXX	Septuagint
NCB	New Century Bible
NIBC	New International Biblical Commentary
NICNT	New International Commentary on the New Testament
NIGTC	New International Greek Text Commentary
NIV	New International Version
NovTest	*Novum Testamentum*
NRSV	New Revised Standard Version
NTS	*New Testament Studies*
SBLDS	Society of Biblical Literature Dissertation Series
SNTSMS	Society for New Testament Studies Monograph Series
WBC	Word Biblical Commentary
ZNW	Zeitschrift für die neutestamentliche Wissenschaft und die Kunde der älteren Kirche

Bibliography

This contains only a brief selection of some of the more significant or helpful books on Hebrews available in English. Short annotations are provided for guidance on the nature of the selected commentaries. For the most part, the titles of the monographs give an indication of the focus of their contributions.

The 'social science' style references in the text and under Further reading are to items listed below. One of the best resources for further material on Hebrews available on the Internet is provided by Dr Mark Goodacre of Duke University through his New Testament Gateway site at http://www.ntgateway.com

Commentaries

Attridge, H. W. (1989) *Hebrews*. Hermeneia; Philadelphia: Fortress. A detailed scholarly commentary that pays particular attention to background sources but is accessible to nonspecialists.

Bruce, F. F. (1990) *The Epistle to the Hebrews* (revised edn). NICNT. Grand Rapids: Eerdmans. First produced in 1963, this commentary provides accessible and solid exegetical analysis.

Buchanan, G. W. (1972) *Hebrews*. AB. New York: Doubleday. Somewhat idiosyncratic in its views of the setting of Hebrews, but worth consulting for its provocative interpretations. Now replaced in the series by Koester (below).

Craddock, F. B. (1998) 'Hebrews', *New Interpreter's Bible XII*. Nashville: Abingdon. pp. 1–174. A readable and reliable brief commentary with helpful sections of theological reflection.

de Silva, D. A. (2000) *Perseverance in Gratitude: A Socio-Rhetorical Commentary on the Epistle 'to the Hebrews'*. Grand Rapids: Eerdmans. A strong all-round commentary which, as its title suggests, pays special attention to social-scientific and rhetorical analysis. It also contains some reflections on contemporary appropriation.

Ellingworth, P. (1993) *The Epistle to the Hebrews: A Commentary on the Greek Text.* NIGTC. Grand Rapids: Eerdmans. Good for detailed linguistic analysis of individual Greek words and phrases.

Gordon, R. P. (2000) *Hebrews.* Readings Commentary. Sheffield: Sheffield Academic Press. A brief, readable commentary providing a helpful orientation to the overall argument of the epistle.

Guthrie, G. H. (1998) *Hebrews.* NIV Application Commentary. Grand Rapids: Zondervan. Based on thorough knowledge of the scholarly literature, this commentary provides the most specific present-day hermeneutical reflection and application for preachers and teachers in the evangelical tradition.

Hagner, D. A. (1990) *Hebrews.* NIBC. Peabody, MA: Hendrickson. A concise and reliable commentary based on the NIV translation.

Heen, E. M. and P. D. W. Krey (eds) (2005) *Hebrews.* Ancient Christian Commentary on Scripture. Leicester: InterVarsity Press. A collection of excerpted comments on the text from selected patristic writers.

Hughes, P. E. (1977) *A Commentary on the Epistle to the Hebrews.* Grand Rapids: Eerdmans. Still worth consulting for its theologically orientated exegesis.

Jewett, R. (1981) *Letter to Pilgrims: A Commentary on the Epistle to the Hebrews.* New York: Pilgrim Press. An interpretation of the epistle in the light of its 'journey' motif and the false teaching addressed in Colossians.

Koester, C. R. (2001) *Hebrews.* AB. New York: Doubleday. Currently the most up-to-date and balanced scholarly commentary, giving attention to a variety of critical approaches and accessible to students without knowledge of Greek.

Lane, W. L. (1991) *Hebrews.* WBC. 2 vols. Dallas: Word. A detailed scholarly commentary on the Greek text that can also be appreciated by students without Greek and is strong on the theological aspects of the letter.

Long, T. G. (1997) *Hebrews.* Interpretation. Louisville: Westminster John Knox. Concise expositions of each pericope with an eye on issues of faith and life in an ecumenical context.

Montefiore, H. W. (1964) *The Epistle to the Hebrews.* BNTC. London: A. and C. Black. A clearly written and accessible commentary, advocating authorship by Apollos.

Pfitzner, V. C. (1997) *Hebrews.* ANTC. Nashville: Abingdon. A compact, reliable and readable commentary.

Westcott, B. F. (1929) *The Epistle to the Hebrews.* London: Macmillan. Completed in 1892, this commentary remains worth consulting for its wise exegesis.

Wilson, R. McL. (1987) *Hebrews.* NCB. London: Marshall, Morgan and Scott. Concise and lucid in its communication of scholarly insights.

Monographs

Cosby, M. R. (1988) *The Rhetorical Composition and Function of Hebrews 11: In Light of Example Lists in Antiquity.* Macon, GA: Mercer University Press.

Croy, N. C. (1998) *Endurance in Suffering. Hebrews 12.1–13 in its Rhetorical, Religious and Philosophical Context.* SNTSMS 98. Cambridge: CUP.

D'Angelo, M. R. (1979) *Moses in the Letter to the Hebrews.* Missoula, MT: Scholars Press.

de Silva, D. A. (1995) *Despising Shame: Honor Discourse and Community Maintenance in the Epistle to the Hebrews.* SBLDS 152. Atlanta: Scholars Press.

Dey, L. K. K. (1975) *Intermediate Patterns of Perfection in Philo and Hebrews.* SBLDS 25. Missoula, MT: Scholars Press.

Dunnill, J. (1992) *Covenant and Sacrifice in the Letter to the Hebrews.* Cambridge: CUP.

Eisenbaum, P. M. (1997) *The Jewish Heroes of Christian History: Hebrews 11 in Literary Context.* Atlanta, GA: SBL.

Gray, P. (2003) *Godly Fear: The Epistle to the Hebrews and Greco-Roman Critiques of Superstition.* Atlanta: SBL.

Guthrie, G. H. (1994) *The Structure of Hebrews: A Text-Linguistic Analysis.* Leiden: E. J. Brill.

Horton, F. L. (1976) *The Melchizedek Tradition: A Critical Examination of the Sources to the Fifth Century A.D. and in the Epistle to the Hebrews.* SNTSMS 30. Cambridge: CUP.

Hughes, G. (1979) *Hebrews and Hermeneutics: The Epistle to the Hebrews as a New Testament Example of Biblical Interpretation.* SNTSMS 36. Cambridge: CUP.

Hurst, L. D. (1990) *The Epistle to the Hebrews: Its Background of Thought.* SNTSMS 65. Cambridge: CUP.

Isaacs, M. E. (1992) *Sacred Space: An Approach to the Theology of the Epistle to the Hebrews.* JSNTSup 73. Sheffield: JSOT Press.

Johnson, R. (2001) *Going Outside the Camp: The Sociological Function of the Levitical Critique in the Epistle to the Hebrews.* JSNTSup 209. London: Sheffield Academic Press.

Käsemann, E. *The Wandering People of God: An Investigation of the Letter to the Hebrews.* Tr. R. Harrisville and I. Sandberg. Minneapolis: Augsburg, 1984. German original 1939.

Kistemaker, S. (1961) *The Psalm Citations in the Epistle to the Hebrews.* Amsterdam: Van Soest.

Lehne, S. (1990) *The New Covenant in Hebrews.* Sheffield: Sheffield Academic Press.

Lindars, B. (1991) *The Theology of the Epistle to the Hebrews.* Cambridge: CUP.

Peterson, D. (1982) *Hebrews and Perfection: An Examination of the Concept of Perfection in the Epistle to the Hebrews.* SNTSMS 47. Cambridge: CUP.

Pursiful, D. J. (1993) *The Cultic Motif in the Spirituality of the Book of Hebrews.* Lewiston, NY: Edwin Mellen.

Rhee, V. (2001) *Faith in Hebrews: Analysis within the Context of Christology, Eschatology and Ethics.* New York: Peter Lang.

Salevao, I. (2002) *Legitimation in the Letter to the Hebrews: The Construction and Maintenance of a Symbolic Universe. JSNTSup* 219. London: Sheffield Academic Press.

Schenk, K. L. (2003) *Understanding the Book of Hebrews*. Louisville: Westminster John Knox.

Scholer, J. M. (1991) *Proleptic Priests: Priesthood in the Epistle to the Hebrews. JSNTSup* 49. Sheffield: Sheffield Academic Press.

Thompson, J. W. (1982) *The Beginnings of Christian Philosophy: The Epistle to the Hebrews*. CBQMS 13. Washington, DC: Catholic Biblical Association.

Trotter, Jr, A. H. (1997) *Interpreting the Epistle to the Hebrews*. Grand Rapids: Baker.

Vanhoye, A. (1989) *Structure and Message of the Epistle to the Hebrews*. Rome: Pontifical Biblical Institute.

Williamson, R. (1970) *Philo and the Epistle to the Hebrews*. Leiden: E. J. Brill.

1

The Place of Hebrews in the Canon
and in the Church

It may seem too obvious to begin with the observation that Hebrews is found toward the back end of the New Testament. Yet noting its place in the sequence of New Testament documents already touches on questions surrounding its original status and on matters affecting its subsequent use. Hebrews comes just after the collection of Pauline letters and, followed by 1–2 Peter, 1–3 John and Jude, is the first of what are frequently called the Catholic epistles. Some editions of the New Testament supply their own headings for its different groups of writings and a standard division is a fourfold one – The Gospels, The Acts of the Apostles, The Letters of Paul, and The General Epistles and Revelation. This fourth grouping often gets short shrift in terms of the amount of attention paid to it by students of the New Testament. Within the grouping the Johannine epistles consistently figure somewhat more prominently, primarily because they are seen as having important links to the Fourth Gospel, and recently, particularly because of the turn of the millennium and the part certain interpretations of Revelation have played on the American political scene, the final book has been in vogue. But in terms of its perceived importance for early Christian thought and its familiarity to present-day students of the New Testament, this group of writings as a whole tends to lose out to the four Gospels and Acts and to the Pauline corpus. This is no less true of Hebrews, despite it being a more substantial document than the other epistles in the group.

In the case of Hebrews, there are additional factors that contribute to its relative neglect. One of these may well be its traditional title – 'The Letter to the Hebrews'. The impact of this title is different from, say, that of 'The Letter to the Philippians'. Present-day readers soon learn to overcome the distancing induced by the latter's geographical designation and begin to realize, if they are Christian readers, that they are able to draw analogies to their own situation from that of the believing inhabitants of Philippi addressed by Paul. But the term 'Hebrews' is an ethnic one and so tends to have a stronger distancing effect on readers who are now likely to be, for the most part, Gentiles. This is reinforced once readers leave behind the somewhat more familiar initial themes of the culmination of prophecy, and the typologies between Moses and Christ and between Israel and believers, and reach the middle of the letter. There the extended discussion of Melchizedek and talk of the details of the tabernacle and cultic arrangements, especially the blood of bulls and goats and the ashes of a heifer (cf. 9.13), reflect the unmistakable difference between the world the writer and first readers inhabited and today's world. Although this difference requires some patient and painstaking negotiation at various points, the good news, as many students discover, is that Hebrews is worth this sort of negotiation and that its writer turns out to be not only the most elegant stylist among the New Testament writers but also a first-class theologian and pastor in his own right, whose message does in fact continue to speak effectively to the church.

The canonical status of Hebrews

The fact that Hebrews is overshadowed by Paul's letters is somewhat ironic, since it was its attribution to Paul in the early stages of the church's life that ensured its place in the canon in the first instance. Its authoritative status became widely recognized when a second-century editor in Alexandria incorporated it into a fourteen-letter Pauline collection. The oldest extant text of Hebrews is in p^{46} (to be dated around 200 CE), which is this collection of Pauline letters, beginning with Romans and placing Hebrews next, presumably on the grounds of length.

Because the recognition of Hebrews as authoritative for the whole church was not an entirely straightforward matter, it is worth tracing briefly at this point some of the stages in its acceptance into the canon. The letter was widely known in the east and west, but had somewhat different reception histories in the two parts of the church. In the west Clement of Rome, around the turn of the century between 90 and 120 CE, made use of Hebrews, taking up some of its words and phrases but without referring to it or its author by name, or calling it Scripture (see *1 Clem.* 9.3, cf. Heb. 11.5; *1 Clem.* 10.7, cf. Heb. 11.17; *1 Clem.* 17.1, cf. Heb. 11.37; *1 Clem.* 21.1, cf. Heb. 12.1; *1 Clem.* 27.2, cf. Heb. 6.18; *1 Clem.* 36.1–6, cf. Heb. 1.3, 4, 7, 13; 2.18; 3.1). The last passage in this list strings together a whole cluster of phrases from Hebrews in depicting Christ as high priest. The Shepherd of Hermas, also written in Rome, between 120 and 140 CE, appears to be acquainted with Hebrews and to be responding to it in its discussion of the possibility of a further repentance after baptism (cf. *Mand.* 4.3.1–2). Justin Martyr (c. 160 CE) employs Hebrews and unusually, as does Heb. 3.1, refers to Christ as apostle (*Apol.*

12.9, 63; see also e.g. *Dial.* 13.1, cf. Heb. 9.13, 14; *Dial.* 19.3, cf. Heb. 11.5; *Dial.* 67.9, cf. Heb. 12.18–21; *Dial.* 96.1, cf. Heb. 7.17, 24; *Dial.* 121.2, cf. Heb. 4.12, 13). Irenaeus, c. 180 CE, (cf. Eusebius, *Hist. eccl.* 5.26.3), Gaius of Rome, c. 200 CE, (cf. Eusebius, *Hist.eccl.* 6.20.3) and Hippolytus, bishop of Rome, c. 200 CE, (*Haer.* 6.30.9) all employed Hebrews but did not ascribe it to Paul.

During the second century, then, Hebrews was widely read and used in the western church, but at this stage and in this area it was deliberately not attributed to Paul. There appears, therefore, to have been an early tradition that the author was someone other than the apostle. Later, in the third century and early part of the fourth, Hebrews appears to have been relatively neglected. This was not only because it was held to be non-Pauline, but probably also because of what was seen as its too rigorous stance in the controversy about post-baptismal repentance, where the western church had adopted the more generous viewpoint of the Shepherd of Hermas. In this regard the differing opinion of Tertullian in North Africa (c. 155–220 CE) is interesting. In his early writings (*Pud.* 20) he opposed the possibility of post-baptismal repentance over against what he called 'that apocryphal Shepherd of Adulterers', cited Heb. 6.4–8, and linked this passage to Barnabas.

The beginning of this discussion of canonical status noted that by the end of the second century, the church in Alexandria did assign Hebrews to Paul. This view was also held more generally in the eastern church. It was known to Pantaenus (c. 180 CE) and his pupil, Clement of Alexandria (c. 200 CE) (cf. Eusebius, *Hist. eccl.* 6.14.1–4). Clement's variation on this view claimed that Paul had originally written the letter in Hebrew, and Luke had translated it into Greek. Taking up a suggestion of Pantaenus, Clement held that Luke had then probably left off Paul's name so as not to offend Jewish Christians who would have been prejudiced against Paul. But there were also some in the east who recognized the authority of Hebrews without attributing Pauline authorship to it. Origen (c. 185–c. 254 CE), for example, noted that 'not without reason the men of old times passed it down as Paul's', that some thought that Clement of Rome wrote it and others Luke, but admitted that, as far as he was concerned, 'who wrote the epistle, in truth God knows' (Eusebius, *Hist.eccl.* 6.25.11–14). Eusebius himself (c. 450 CE), though he was aware of the issues surrounding authorship, included Hebrews among the fourteen letters of Paul (*Hist. eccl.* 3.3.5; 6.20.3), as did Athanasius in his Festal Letter of 367 CE (*Ep. fest.* 39.5), placing it after Paul's letters to churches and before the letters to individuals. The latter position is also where Hebrews is found in the major codices (Sinaiticus, Alexandrinus, Vaticanus) that date from the fourth and fifth centuries.

Towards the end of the fourth century, after there had been a period of increased contact and exchange of views, a consensus was established between east and west that Hebrews be included in the list of authoritative documents as the fourteenth of the Pauline letters. This stance can be found in *De Trin.* 4.11 by Hilary of Poitiers (c. 315–367 CE) and, more decisively for the views of the western church, is attested in the writings of Jerome, c. 342–420 CE (*Vir. ill.* 5; *Epist.* 53.8; 129.3) and of Augustine, 354–430 CE (*Doctr. chr.* 2.8; *Civ.* 16.22). The last two make clear that they are aware of the problem of authorship but nevertheless treat Hebrews as authoritative. Jerome (*Epist.* 129), written in 414 CE, states, 'The Epistle which is inscribed to the Hebrews is received not only by the Churches of the East, but also by all Church writers of the Greek language before our days, as of Paul the apostle, though many think it is from Barnabas or Clement. And it makes no difference whose it is, since it is from a churchman, and is celebrated in the daily readings of the Churches.' Augustine starts out by quoting from Hebrews as one of Paul's writings until 406 CE, then becomes more hesitant, and ends up after 409 CE by citing it anonymously. By the time of the Synod of Hippo in 393 CE and the Synods of Carthage in 397 and 419 CE Hebrews was part of the canonical list but the caution over its Pauline authorship is reflected in its being appended to the end of the Pauline letter collection, which is the position it has in D, a codex from the sixth century, in E K L from the ninth century and in most minuscules and which it has retained in nearly all texts of the New Testament since that time.

As the quotation above from Jerome indicates, catholicity or wide usage served as one of the criteria for canonicity, and despite its chequered career, Hebrews did relatively well on that score. But apostolicity was also a criterion. This was not taken in its strictest sense but rather entailed being recognized as in line with and conveying the apostolic teaching. Nevertheless, as far as possible, the second and third century churches wanted also to be able to attach to a writing an apostolic name or the name of an apostolic associate, such as Luke, in order to guarantee its apostolicity. So it is not surprising that in the case of Hebrews, where the author does not state his or her name in the opening address, the matter of authorship became closely tied to the issue of canonicity. From a much later perspective the usual judgement has been that authorship and authority became confused on the part of some but, in the providence of God, the church catholic rightly heard in Hebrews the apostolic gospel that witnessed powerfully to God's decisive action in Christ and to its implications for faith and life. Although a large part of that church was mistaken in thinking that this quality was dependent on Pauline authorship, in the end Hebrews was recognized as authoritative in the evident awareness that there were problems with attaching Paul's name to it.

Later reception of Hebrews

As has been noted, in the early period the evaluation of Hebrews was affected by attitudes to post-baptismal sin. The equivalent issue that came to the fore particularly during the Reformation period was whether Christian believers could fall away from grace and become apostate. Luther, who had some idiosyncratic views about particular New Testament books, reckoned that Hebrews was unapostolic and contained some 'wood, straw or hay' mingled with 'gold, silver and precious stones'. He therefore relegated the epistle to the end of his New Testament (cf. his preface to Hebrews in 1522 in J. Pelikan and H. Lehman (eds), *Luther's Works*, Vol. 35, Philadelphia: Fortress, 1960, pp. 394–95). He came to this judgement primarily because he thought that the strong words of Hebrews 6 about the impossibility of restoring again to repentance those who have once been enlightened and then fallen away conflicted with his central conviction about the availability of God's grace in Christ through faith. Yet Calvin, who also stated that Paul was not the author, had a very different and much more representative view. In the 'Introduction' to his commentary of 1549 he could write, 'I class it without hesitation among the apostolical [that is, authoritative] writings . . . There is, indeed, no book in Holy Scripture which speaks so clearly of the priesthood of Christ, which so highly exalts the virtue and dignity of that only true sacrifice which he offered by his death, which so abundantly deals with the use of ceremonies as well as their abrogation, and, in a word, which so fully explains that Christ is the end of the law. Let us, therefore, not allow the church of God or ourselves to be deprived of so great a benefit, but firmly defend the possession of it' (*The Epistle of Paul the Apostle to the Hebrews and the First and Second Epistles of St. Peter*, tr. W. B. Johnston; Edinburgh: Oliver and Boyd, 1963, p. 1). Calvin was clearly able to find ways to reconcile the language of Hebrews' severe warnings with his beliefs about God's grace and the perseverance of the saints. Nevertheless, the issue of whether it is possible for one who has truly believed in Christ irrevocably to fall away rumbled on. It continues into the present in some circles, as Heb. 6.4–8 and 10.26–31 fuel disputes between Christians from more Reformed traditions who emphasize God's initiative in salvation and those of more Arminian persuasion who stress human free will.

But interpreters of Hebrews have not simply worried about its warnings and their implications. They have also drawn comfort and assurance from its portrait of Christ. The threefold categorization of Christ as prophet, priest and king has a long history and for the second category Hebrews has obviously been the main New Testament resource. Its depiction of Christ as heavenly high priest who intercedes sympathetically and effectively for believers has had a lasting impact. This portrayal of Christ's high priesthood and of the 'once-for-all' nature of his sacrificial death has, however, from time to time also provoked debate between more Protestant and more Catholic readers. At issue has been whether the representation of Christ as high priest supports or undermines the tradition of viewing clergy as priests, and whether the notion of offering the elements in the eucharist as a sacrifice of Christ's body is compatible with the stress on the finality of Christ's death as sacrifice in Hebrews.

The problem of the interpretation by a largely Gentile church of a document whose heading suggests it was originally written for Jewish readers has already been raised. The second half of the twentieth century has seen this matter surface in two different ways. On the one hand, there has been the growth of a group of Christians who have taken a renewed interest in this letter, namely Messianic Jews, of whom 'Jews for Jesus' is one well-known and sometimes controversial strand. Such Jewish Christians have found Hebrews a rich resource in developing their own distinctive identity and in formulating their witness to fellow Jews. On the other hand, some non-Christian Jews and many Christians, sensitive to anti-Semitism and to the horrors of the Holocaust, have been greatly troubled by what they see as the anti-Judaism of much of the New Testament. Hebrews has not escaped their indictment and its supersessionist treatment of the 'old covenant' has been deemed responsible for helping to engender among Christians a disparaging attitude to ongoing forms of Judaism. This is a topic that continues to attract discussion in academic New Testament scholarship, and we shall need to return to it later.

During the last century, however, most of the debates surrounding Hebrews within academic scholarship have been on relatively less significant matters. Does its world of thought owe more to Gnosticism, to Jewish apocalyptic writings or to some form of Platonism? Was its intended audience composed of Jewish or Gentile Christians, or both? Is it a unified composition, or was chapter 13 added later? How does its treatment of Scriptural texts compare with the techniques used by other first-century Jewish writers? Although some outstanding commentaries have been produced on this letter, it has never sparked major controversy in the same way as study of the historical Jesus or of the genre, historicity and theology of the Gospels or of issues in Pauline theology, but has remained quietly in the background. Perhaps more surprisingly, this background role is also reflected in many of the books that have been produced on New Testament theology. With very few exceptions, the space given to the thought of Hebrews is extremely limited and one would have little idea that its author arguably ranks alongside Paul and the author of the Fourth Gospel in terms of the creativity and profundity of his theologizing. In systematic theologies that interact with Scripture in any major way, Hebrews occasionally features but, not surprisingly, its treatment is largely confined to discussions of the atonement and attempts to elucidate the sacrificial metaphor for Christ's death (cf. e.g. K. Barth, *Church Dogmatics* IV/1, Edinburgh: T & T Clark, 1956, pp. 273–83).

Among Christians more generally it would probably be fair to say that most are familiar only with particular texts or passages from Hebrews. Prominent among such texts would be 'For the word of God is living and active, sharper than any two-edged sword' (4.12) or 'Jesus Christ is the same yesterday and today and forever' (13.8), and among better-known passages would be the list of the heroes and heroines of faith (11.1–40). The language of 'approaching the throne of grace with boldness' (4.16) is sometimes taken up in prayers, while 'Now may the God of peace, who brought back from the dead our Lord Jesus, the great shepherd of the sheep, by the blood of the eternal covenant, make you complete in everything good so that you may do his will, working among us that which is pleasing in his sight, through Jesus Christ, to whom be the glory for ever and ever. Amen' (13.20, 21) is frequently pronounced as a benediction in worship.

Although their source may not always be recognized, other phrases or images from Hebrews have found their way into some of the church's classic hymns. The language of taking refuge (6.18) and the promise 'I will never leave you nor forsake you' (13.5) are taken up in 'How firm a foundation', which contains the lines – 'What more can He say than to you He hath said, You who unto Jesus for refuge have fled' and 'That soul, though all hell should endeavour to shake, He never will leave, He will never forsake.' The hymn 'My hope is built' employs the notions of oath, hope, anchor, soul and veil or curtain (6.17–19): 'In every high and stormy gale My anchor holds within the veil. His oath, his covenant, and blood, Support me in the whelming flood; When all around my soul gives way, He then is all my hope and stay.'

Hebrews also features in a major way in the worship of many churches through its place in the lectionary readings. In the three-year cycle of *The Revised Common Lectionary* Hebrews provides the reading from the epistle on Monday (Heb. 9.11–15), Wednesday (Heb. 12.1–3) and Good Friday (either Heb. 10.16–25 or Heb. 4.14–16; 5.7–9) of Holy Week each year. In addition, in the second year between Pentecost and Advent there are epistle readings for five Sundays containing excerpts from Heb. 1, 2, 4, 5, 7, 9, and in the third year for four Sundays containing passages from Heb. 11–13. So this epistle is not unrepresented, but since Hebrews is one sustained and extended argument, the fragmentary nature of the lectionary selection does not necessarily afford the best opportunity for becoming acquainted with its overall message.

Many involved in study of the New Testament would also be hard put to summarize the thought and purposes of Hebrews. This Guide is intended to help to remedy that situation and to enable a greater appreciation of the distinctive voice of Hebrews within the New Testament canon. Some of the features of Hebrews' distinctiveness can be highlighted in anticipation of the fuller discussion. This epistle contributes its own perspective on how Jesus Christ is to be seen as both fully human and divine. It stresses the once-for-all nature of his death and its achievement and adds to other models for the atonement its own development of cultic and sacrificial imagery. It focuses in a special way on the exaltation, rather than the resurrection, of Christ and on the resultant opening up of heavenly realities for believers. It provides some of the most profound reflection on the relationships between the old covenant and the new and between the Jewish Scriptures and the decisive word God has spoken in Christ. It emphasizes the significance of faith and hope and the urgency of continuing in commitment to Christ, and it depicts Christian existence in terms of confident worship and persevering pilgrimage in a community that is able to face persecution and death as it follows the one who has already pioneered the way.

Further reading

On the formation of the canon, see B. M. Metzger (1987) *The Canon of the New Testament. Its Origin, Development and Significance* (Oxford: Clarendon).

For some interpretations of Hebrews from the early period of church history, see Heen and Krey 2005.

For a survey of the history of the interpretation and influence of Hebrews, see Koester 2001:19–63.

For hymns related to Hebrews, see http://www.cyberhymnal.org/scr/scriptur.htm

2

Genre and Rhetoric

The original superscription or heading attached to this document at an early stage read simply 'To the Hebrews'. Most English translations of the New Testament have extended the heading by prefixing to it either 'The Letter' or 'The Epistle', and this is how we have referred to Hebrews up to this point. Such a heading leads readers familiar with the preceding Pauline letters to expect a writing that takes the same overall shape as the written communications from the apostle to the Gentiles. They immediately discover from the beginning of Hebrews, which contains no address to recipients, that this is not the case. So is Hebrews perhaps not best described as a letter? In attempting to persuade his readers of his message, what form of communication does the writer employ and how might a consideration of the genre of Hebrews aid appreciation of its writer's concerns and his relationship to his addressees?

A word of exhortation

The writer's own description of his communication is 'a word of exhortation' (13.22). He does not, however, claim exclusive rights to this activity of exhortation. In fact, he expects all the hearers or readers of his message to be regularly engaged in it. In 3.13 he writes, 'But exhort one another every day, as long as it is called "today", so that none of you may be hardened by the deceitfulness of sin', and later in 10.24, 25 he talks of them provoking one another to love and good works, by not neglecting to meet together and by 'encouraging one another'. In this second reference 'encouraging' (NRSV) translates the same Greek verb (*parakaleō*) that is rendered as 'exhort' in the first reference and that has as its cognate noun the term used of the writing as a whole in 13.22.

What is the force of this Greek word group? Depending on the context, it can have the force of summoning, appealing to, urging, imploring, exhorting, encouraging, comforting or admonishing. The verb is employed to introduce the sections of ethical exhortation or paraenesis in Pauline letters (cf. Rom. 12.1; 1 Thess. 4.1; Phil. 4.2, cf. also Eph. 4.1), where it functions to urge or admonish believers to forms of conduct appropriate to the gospel message. The noun is used earlier in Hebrews in 6.18, where the writer argues that through God's promise and oath 'we . . . might have strong encouragement to seize the hope set before us' (author's translation). In Heb. 12.5, 6 the quotation from Prov. 3.11 is introduced by 'you have forgotten the exhortation . . .'. The quotation itself asserts, 'Do not lose heart', and the writer explains that the discipline or correction of which it speaks is a sign of being legitimate children and not bastards. So this exhortation amounts to an encouragement. At the end of Hebrews in 13.19 the verb from the word group introduces the exhortation to pray, and then in 13.22 both the verb and the noun are found in a sentence exhorting the addressees to bear with the writer's exhortation! When, then, in this verse the whole communication is described as a word of exhortation, in the light of the earlier usage of the 'exhorting' word group and of the content of its message, that communication can be understood as having been intended to urge and admonish its readers in such a way as to encourage them to hold fast to their Christian confession and to pursue the sort of life that is appropriate to such a confession.

A sermon or homily

In composing his exhortation, the writer is only doing in a heightened and more extended fashion what he expects every member of the community to do. But when exhortation takes on this lengthier (though in 13.22 the writer says that he has been brief!) and more elaborate form, then 'word of exhortation' can have a semi-technical sense in which it refers to a discourse spoken by teachers or prophets in the community. In the context of the synagogue such a discourse took the form of a homily or sermon. This is precisely what Luke depicts when in Acts 13.15 he has Paul give an address in the synagogue service at Pisidian Antioch. After the reading of the law and the prophets, the synagogue officials ask Paul and his companions whether they have any 'word of exhortation' (the same phrase as in Heb. 13.22) for the people, and so Paul stands up and gives an extended discourse. It involves an account of Israel's history that includes a Scriptural quotation; it links this history to Christ as its fulfilment; it proclaims the gospel, again showing Christ to be the fulfilment of God's promises and of specific Scriptures; and it concludes in 13.40, 41 with an admonition using the words of a further Scriptural text (Hab. 1.5) – 'Beware therefore that what the prophets said does not happen to you: "Look, you scoffers! Be amazed and perish, for in your days I am doing a work, a work that you will never believe, even if someone tells you."' In its use of Scripture, its linkage to Christ and its application in an exhortation to its hearers, this synagogue homily is not dissimilar to Hebrews.

Various writers on Hebrews have in fact from time to time suggested that it was a sermon. This proposal was put on a firmer footing by the German scholar, H. Thyen (*Der Stil der Jüdisch-Hellenistischen Homilie*, Göttingen: Vandenhoeck and Ruprecht, 1955), who examined a number of writings that he put into the category of Jewish Hellenistic homilies and then claimed that the bulk of Hebrews is a carefully constructed homily of the type given in a diaspora synagogue. His work is summarized and briefly evaluated by Swetnam (1969). Thyen pointed to such matters as the author's command of diverse rhetorical devices; his frequent change from 'we' to 'you' to 'I'; his remarkable knowledge and use of the Septuagint (LXX), where citations from the Pentateuch and the Psalms predominate; his method of citation, especially introducing quotations with 'and again' (cf. 1.5; 2.13 (2x); 4.5; 10.30), 'also in another place' (cf. 5.6) and a rhetorical question (cf. 1.5); and his ending with a series of admonitions (cf. Heb. 12–13). It has been pointed out, however, that many of these features would not be restricted to diaspora synagogue homilies but would be characteristic of any synagogue homily in Greek, even in Palestine.

Wills (1984), in a further analysis of Hellenistic Jewish and early Christian sermonic discourses, claimed that they exhibited a distinctive threefold pattern: (i) the presentation of authoritative examples, most frequently biblical ones, accompanied by biblical quotations and reasoned exposition of theological points; (ii) a conclusion based on the preceding examples and commentary, indicating their significance for those addressed; and (iii) a final exhortation based on the preceding conclusion. In the light of these findings, Wills held that Hebrews had adapted this pattern and given it more sophistication in its complex sermonic text.

Despite its final written form, some of the oral features one would find in a sermon still appear in Hebrews. In particular, the uses of verbs for speaking, where in a written composition one would have expected verbs for writing, are striking. Examples include 2.5: 'Now God did not subject the coming world, about which we are speaking, to angels'; 5.11: 'About this we have much to say that is hard to explain'; 6.9: 'Even though we speak in this way, beloved . . .'; 8.1: 'Now the main point in what we are saying is this . . .'; 9.5: 'Of these things we cannot now speak in detail'; 11.32: 'And what more should I say? For time would fail me to tell of Gideon, Barak . . .'.

A sermon based on Scripture

If a 'word of exhortation' could refer to a synagogue homily and if, like that depicted in Acts 13, such a homily followed on from the reading of the law and the prophets, then it would have midrashic features. The term 'midrash' can be used to describe a general technique for interpreting Scripture, or the resultant work of interpretation. In the latter sense a midrash is a commentary on a Scriptural text, an exposition that wove aspects of this text and of other texts into its interpretation. The purpose of employing midrash as a technique was to facilitate the Scriptural text's meaning for and application to the current situation of its hearers. Before beginning its commentary, midrash proper always cited the main Scriptural text first, but midrash could also take a more implicit form in which the text for the day or the major text would be assumed rather than formally cited. The underlying text would become apparent from its elements and motifs that appeared in the commentary material. A typical sermon in midrashic form would include the following: (i) the text for the day (usually from the Pentateuch), (ii) a second text to introduce the discourse, (iii) exposition (containing additional scriptural citation, parables or other means of commentary, and linked to the initial texts by catchwords), and (iv) a final text (usually repeating or at least alluding to the text for the day).

As a sermon that involves extensive use of Scripture, Hebrews also has prominent midrashic features both in individual sections and in the whole composition. One longer section that serves as an example is 10.5–39. This passage employs Ps. 40.6–8 as its initial text in vv. 5–7. In citing the scriptural text, the author uses the LXX, which has changed the original Hebrew wording of 'ears you have prepared for me' to 'a body you have prepared for me'. The latter rendering is clearly more appropriate for what will be said about Christ in the commentary in v. 10. This text is then followed by the exposition of vv. 8–36, which begins with commentary from v. 8 onward and then brings in additional citations and allusions. Exod. 29.38 is taken up in v. 11, Ps. 110.1 in vv. 12, 13, Jer. 31.33, 34 in vv. 16, 17, Isa. 26.11 in v. 27, Deut. 17.6 and 19.15 in v. 28, Exod. 24.8 in v. 29, and Deut. 32.35, 36 in v. 30. The exposition also contains links back to the initial text through catchwords, e.g. 'sacrifice' (vv. 8, 11, 12, 26), 'offering' (vv. 8, 10, 14, 18), 'for sin' (vv. 8, 18, 26), 'sin/sins' (vv. 11, 12, 17), and 'will/ God's will' (vv. 9, 10, 36). The exposition is rounded off with more direct application in vv. 32–36. Finally, there is a concluding Scriptural text, together with its application, in vv. 37–39. This is a combination of Isa. 26.20 and Hab. 2.3, 4 and refers back to the initial text through the terms 'come' (cf. 'I have come' in v. 7) and 'takes no pleasure' (cf. 'have taken no pleasure' in v. 6).

But if the whole of Hebrews is a synagogue homily, then arguably its sermon can be seen to be an implicit midrash woven around Ps. 110.1, 4. Buchanan (1972) made a similar suggestion in his commentary, although he pressed it too hard and also described Hebrews as a 'homiletical midrash'. In the light of what has been said about midrash, it would be more accurate to designate it a 'midrashic homily'. Certainly the two verses from the psalm contain the major theme of Hebrews – the exaltation of Christ at God's right hand (Ps. 110.1) and specifically his exaltation as priest after the order of Melchizedek according to God's oath (Ps. 110.4). It is significant that 8.1, a key text in Hebrews, puts its summary of the overall message in terms of these two verses – 'Now the point in what we are saying is this: we have such a high priest [i.e. one after the order of Melchizedek, who has just been discussed] (Ps. 110.4), one who is seated at the right hand of the throne of the Majesty in heaven (Ps. 110.1).' Not only do the psalm verses provide the theme of the writer's message, they also feature throughout the homily. Ps. 110.1 figures right at the sermon's beginning; its wording is clearly alluded to in the prologue or exordium in 1.3, and then it is actually cited in 1.13. Ps. 110.4 is quoted for the first time in 5.6, alluded to both in terms of the Melchizedek high priesthood and God's oath throughout chs 5–7 (cf. 5.10; 6.17, 20; 7.3, 11, 15, 20, 24, 28) and explicitly cited twice in this section in 7.17, 21. Then, as has been noted, the two psalm verses are combined in the wording of 8.1 before Ps. 110.1 is cited again twice in 10.12, 13 and picked up as a motif at the beginning of the final paraenesis in 12.2. Taken together, the two psalm verses function as the implicit main text for the whole communication.

A written sermon sent as a letter

This discussion has focused first on the homiletical aspects of Hebrews as distinctive of its genre because, although it is commonly called a letter or epistle, it does not, as noted earlier, have some of the main features of a letter that are associated with the Pauline correspondence. Most strikingly, it does not begin with epistolary conventions. There is no address from the writer to the readers, no opening salutation, and no intercessory prayer report or thanksgiving period, signalling the concerns of the writer. Instead it begins immediately with its subject matter. Yet Hebrews does end as a letter. The benediction of 13.20, 21, which forms an effective ending to the homily, was also a part of the closing elements of early Christian letters. It is followed by other such elements – a final word of exhortation (13.22), news of a fellow Christian, Timothy, known to writer and addressees, and travel plans (13.23), greetings (13.24) and a final grace benediction (13.25). Its only partial epistolary form has been dubbed the 'literary puzzle' of Hebrews, particularly by W. Wrede (*Das literarische Rätsel des Hebräerbriefes*, Göttingen: Vandenhoeck and Ruprecht, 1906). Wrede himself held that the writer started out to produce a homily but then changed his mind and in chapter 13 began to turn the writing into an epistle. Finally, he decided to attempt to give the epistle an authentic Pauline flavour, so he added a second conclusion in 13.22–25, in which he was influenced by Phil. 2.19–24, a passage in which Paul wrote about sending Timothy and about hoping to come soon himself. But on this view it is strange that such an accomplished writer did not do rather better with the 'Pauline' ending. The wording is not at all close to Phil. 2.19–24, and the conclusion could have been made much more obviously Pauline than simply containing a reference to Timothy.

Actually, once it is granted that the writer knows his addressees and is prevented by absence from delivering his homily in person, the epistolary conclusion makes good sense. Wrede may well be right that the epistolary form comes into play from the beginning of ch. 13, although this does not require one to speculate that this entailed a change of mind on the part of the writer. Chapter 13 contains the kind of miscellaneous exhortations found in the closing paraenesis of other letters and, toward the end of his, this writer makes clear that he has written down his preceding homily for the intended audience – 'bear with my word of exhortation, for I have written to you briefly' (13.22). It would be natural at that point to add brief personal details and greetings and to round off the whole with a grace benediction in the way typical of other early Christian written communications. A dissenting view has recently been proposed by Wedderburn (2004: 390–406), who argues that chapter 13 is different enough from the rest of the letter to be assigned to a different author writing to a different situation.

The discussion of the document's genre to this point leads to the following conclusion. Hebrews is a word of exhortation, a midrashic sermon based on Scripture, particularly Ps. 110.1, 4, sent in written form (as a substitute for its author's personal presence) to a community known to him, and for this reason it ends with miscellaneous exhortations followed by the other elements which conform to the conventions of an epistolary conclusion.

Elements of Graeco-Roman rhetoric

Like most sermons, this one seeks to persuade its hearers and as such it is a piece of rhetoric. Not only is its writer well versed in the Greek version of the Jewish Scriptures, he also has a more than passing acquaintance with the conventions of Greek rhetoric. Aune (1987) can assert, 'The author obviously enjoyed the benefits of a Hellenistic rhetorical education through the tertiary level' (p. 212). It is appropriate, then, to attempt to analyse the sermon in terms of the rhetorical practices of the time. In doing so, the following questions are pertinent. What is its rhetorical situation, that is, what issue or difficulty for the audience is it attempting to address through its methods of persuasion? Does it belong to any of the three major rhetorical genres and, if so, which? Does it exemplify the three main features of ancient rhetoric – ethos, pathos and logos – and, if so, how? More specifically, does it have the structural divisions one would expect in a rhetorical discourse and what techniques does it employ?

Rhetorical situation

The rhetorical situation is technically called the *stasis*, the basis of the problem being addressed. Discovering this entails isolating what the writer sees as the main issue to be met if his persuasion is to be effective, what he views as the obstacle to be overcome if the audience is to be convinced. Later, more detailed discussion of the setting and purposes of Hebrews in Chapter 5 will obviously have a major bearing on this question. In anticipation of that discussion one could say briefly at this point that the writer sees the audience as in danger, because of various factors, of giving up their Christian confession, and so he wants to dissuade them from doing so. Put positively, he wants to persuade them to hold firm to their Christian confession, not drifting away or shrinking back but living out its consequences confidently by enduring whatever hostility it may provoke from others. In order for his message to be effective, he also thinks that its recipients need a clearer understanding that what God has now done in Christ is superior to previous forms of revelation and has an aspect of finality about it.

Rhetorical genre

The three main types of ancient rhetoric were *judicial*, *deliberative*, and *epideictic* rhetoric. *Judicial* rhetoric is concerned with accusation and defence, setting out what is the case and what is just or unjust. It does not apply to Hebrews, which is not an apologetic discourse. *Deliberative* rhetoric is concerned with persuasion and dissuasion, urging the audience to take or not to take a particular course of action in the future. It emphasizes what is advantageous or harmful. This category, then, does appear to be relevant to Hebrews. *Epideictic* rhetoric praises and blames, concerns itself with what is honourable or dishonourable, and does so with the aim of increasing or decreasing assent and adherence to certain values. This also appears to match at least part of the purpose of Hebrews. It would not be unusual to find two of these categories relevant, since a discourse could often involve a combination of rhetorical genres. Nevertheless, one would be likely to be the predominant category with the other in a supporting role.

Scholars have differed on which genre predominates in Hebrews. Attridge (1989:14) claims, 'it is clearly an epideictic oration, celebrating the significance of Christ and inculcating values that his followers ought to share'. Lindars (1989) is equally sure Hebrews is deliberative, seeing it as an attempt to persuade the audience of Jewish Christians, who are driven by a guilty conscience because of sin, to return to the apostolic faith after it had turned to Judaism to find purification. The decision one comes to on this issue depends on how one relates the two types of argument that are found in Hebrews – the more theological exposition showing the superiority of what God has accomplished in Christ, and the hortatory material with which it is interspersed. The former, in its praise of Jesus' status and achievements, is epideictic and concerned to produce adherence to the confession about him. The latter, with its attempt to dissuade readers from falling away and to persuade them to appropriately Christian attitudes and actions, is deliberative in its orientation. However, these are not simply two separate blocks of material within the sermon. Instead, the exposition continually leads to exhortation and the exhortation is built on the preceding exposition. In this way the epideictic material is in fact in the service of the deliberative. The writer is primarily concerned about the future course of action of his audience and employs his theological arguments, which are meant to reinforce their wavering convictions, as a means to ensure that they avoid actions that will entail ultimate danger in terms of judgement, and that they pursue conduct that will instead be pleasing to God.

More specific rhetorical analogies and divisions

Other more specific suggestions about the document's rhetorical genre fail to convince. Olbricht (1993) holds that Hebrews is modelled on the ancient funeral oration, where comparisons of the deceased with illustrious figures of the past were made in order to praise the superiority of the deceased. This praise treated noteworthy aspects of the subject's life (nobility of birth and ancestors, education, achievements, death) and his or her physical attributes and moral qualities, especially as the latter were displayed in actions that benefited others. A number of these topics do feature in Hebrews' encomium of Jesus, but the discourse as a whole cannot be pressed into this mould without distortion, especially since it contains so much stress on the present exalted life and ministry of Christ. W. G. Übelacker (*Der Hebräerbrief als Appell: Untersuchungen zu exordium, narratio und postscriptum (Hebr 1–2 und 13, 22–25)*, Stockholm: Almqvist and Wiksell, 1989) agrees with the conclusion reached above that the genre is deliberative and then goes on to claim that it is possible to outline the discourse with all the major rhetorical divisions. His proposal has 1.1–4 as the *exordium* (the introduction that attempts to make the audience well-disposed to the message), 1.5–2.18

as the *narratio* (the narration of the pertinent facts) culminating in 2.17, 18 as the *propositio* (the stating of the topic to be discussed), the long section consisting of 3.1–12.29 as the *argumentatio*, presenting the main argument and including *probatio*, the proof of the speaker's case, and *refutatio*, the disproof of an opposing case, 13.1–21 as the *peroratio* (the recapitulation of the main points with a final appeal to the audience's emotions), and 13.22–25 as the *postscriptum*, the postscript. In response to Übelacker's analysis, it can be said that 1.1–4 works well as the *exordium*. 2.17, 18 is certainly the first mention of the main topic of the argument, the high priesthood of Christ, but 1.5–2.18 does not read at all like a setting out of facts in sequence. Instead, it is not dissimilar to the sort of material found in his *argumentatio*. Though there are one or two elements in 13.1–21 that pick up on the previous argument, it scarcely functions as an explicit recapitulation, introduces too many new topics into its exhortations, and is too long to form the effective *peroratio* advocated by ancient rhetorical theorists. As will be seen, 12.18–29 has a better claim to be the *peroratio*. It seems wiser, then, to recognize the discourse as deliberative, to be alert to how its sections function rhetorically within the discourse, especially the beginning (in 1.1–4) and the end (in 12.18–29), and to be aware that as yet no one has shown that the various elements of its major part, the *argumentatio*, conform more precisely to the divisions of a Graeco-Roman discourse. Indeed its distinctive working with Scripture, its patterns of interrelating exposition and exhortation and its pastoral aims may well mean that there is no attempt to follow such divisions in the body of the discourse. Instead it is, as has been claimed, a sermon, but one whose overall shape possesses features recognizable from Graeco-Roman rhetorical conventions.

Ethos, pathos and logos

In discussions of ancient rhetoric ethos refers to the character of the speaker demonstrated in the discourse, and this is utilized to enhance the persuasive force of his argument. Pathos indicates the arousal of the audience's emotions in favour of the position being advocated by the speaker. Logos is the reasoned argument of the discourse, using such means as induction, deduction, and proofs from example. An examination of each of these features illuminates the argument of Hebrews.

(i) Ethos

In this rhetorical discourse the speaker reveals very little of himself by means of personal details, most obviously not even revealing his name. He does not have to do so, because he is already known to the hearers. He is able simply to assume the right to address the audience with his

exhortation and the likelihood that the hearers will accept this interven-
tion (cf. 13.22). This suggests that he has a recognized teaching role, in
all probability one that he has already exercised among them. He refers to
this role as teacher in 5.11–14, where he also admonishes them for having
become dull in understanding. But he does not simply impose his teaching and admonition on them authoritatively. The paraenetical sections
show that he knows and enters into their situation, and this pastoral sensitivity colours his teaching. Even after issuing a warning in the strongest
terms, he can then, in order to reassure them, state that he is basically confident about their salvation (6.9, 10; 10.39). He shows his solidarity with
his audience by employing 'we' predominantly (cf. e.g. 2.1–3; 3.6; 4.1–3;
10.23, 24), though he can also use 'you' in direct address. He also aligns
himself with them when he solicits their prayers that he be restored to
them soon (13.18, 19), and that latter thought, together with the mention
of coming to them in 13.23, conveys not only his concern for the audience
but also his desire to be with them in person. At the end also he speaks of
his good or clear conscience and his honorable motives or desire to act
commendably in all things (13.18), thereby recommending himself but
without any undue boasting. He simply indicates that, in regard to his
attitude and actions towards them, he himself exemplifies qualities that he
has earlier affirmed (cf. 10.22, 24).

(ii) Pathos

The writer clearly wishes to arouse feelings of admiration for and devo-
tion to Christ by depicting Christ throughout the discourse as superior
to all previous forms of God's revelation. This will have been aided if, as
seems likely, right at the beginning he employs traditional worship
material already known to them (cf. 1.2, 3). He also stirs feelings of sympathy for and solidarity with Christ as he depicts him having been tested
through suffering (2.18), particularly when he talks of his loud cries and
tears in the face of death (5.7). At the same time he wants to make the
readers sense the danger and awfulness of going back on their confession, so he talks of the impossibility of being restored again to repentance
and of the possibility of crucifying again the Son of God and holding
him up to contempt (6.4–6). He tries to inspire a dread of judgement
and a proper sense of fear for the God with whom they have to do
(10.26–31; 12.25–29). Yet, alongside this emphasis, there is the repeated
attempt to kindle feelings of confidence before God on the basis of
Christ's work (3.6; 4.16; 7.25; 10.19–22) and to arouse a sense of
worship and of gratitude (12.22–24, 28; 13.15). By recalling earlier days
when his readers had endured suffering successfully, he hopes to touch a
chord that will encourage them to persevere (10.32–35). His listing of
heroes and heroines is designed to inspire and to stir admiration that

will lead the audience, who are in a more advantageous position in terms of God's promises, to emulate their faith (11.4–12.2). His recalling the former leaders of the community is intended to evoke similar emotions (13.7).

(iii) *Logos*

The content and style of the argument will be treated in more detail later. It is sufficient here to point out again that in large part the argument is built up by means of quotation of and reflection on Scripture, which uses the variety of exegetical techniques to be found in the midrashic commenting of the time. But, more than that, the argument proceeds by repeatedly first laying an expositional and theological foundation and then moving, on the basis of that foundation, to exhortation. If such and such is the case theologically, so the pattern of the argument indicates, then here is what should follow in terms of attitude and behaviour.

Specific rhetorical arguments and techniques

Some of the more prominent of the writer's specific types of argument and rhetorical techniques should be mentioned briefly here. Trotter (1997: 67–75, 164–77) provides a listing and discussion of some of those featured below and also of others, such as diatribe and rhythm.

(i) *Synkrisis*

This is a major aspect of the argument of Hebrews. What has traditionally been described in terms of showing the superiority of Christ to older forms of revelation is seen in rhetorical terms as an example of *synkrisis*, a rhetorical form that compares representatives of a type in order to determine the superiority of one over another. It functions as a means of praise or blame by comparison and makes the comparison in terms of family, natural endowments, education, achievements and death. In Hebrews various earlier figures or types of Christ are seen as lesser by comparison with him, and family relations (Christ as the divine Son), education (learning perfection through suffering), and death (the achievement of Christ's sacrificial death) all feature in the comparison. This sort of argument structures the discourse because, as in an encomium, a discourse in praise of someone, the *synkrisis* is used for the purpose of moral exhortation. So in Hebrews, the comparison of angels and the Son, of Moses and Christ, of Aaron and Christ, of the levitical priesthood and Christ, of the old covenant and the new covenant, is in each case followed by paraenesis. Comparison also involves, of course, the type of argument that moves from the lesser to the greater. This can take the form of 'if . . . how much more/less . . .' (cf. 9.13, 14; 12.25, 26).

(ii) Amplification

This rhetorical technique, based on patterns of parallelism and development, produces a certain redundancy of style and would have suggested to
hearers or readers a grandeur of treatment appropriate to the consideration
of lofty or divine themes. The variety of ways in which the theme of Christ
as high priest is developed is one obvious example of this. The writer is
not content to state the theme once, draw some implications and move
on. Instead this theme is amplified in different ways. To take just the first
part of the development, Christ is introduced as a 'merciful and faithful
high priest in the service of God' (2.17), then called 'the high priest of our
confession' (3.1) and 'a great high priest who has passed through the
heavens' (4.14), then compared with other high priests in terms of the
necessary qualifications (5.1–10) before being designated 'a high priest
according to the order of Melchizedek' (5.10).

(iii) Anaphora

This involves repetition of a word or words in successive units of speech,
and can be seen as a more specific aspect of amplification. Examples
include the threefold use of the phrase 'for ever' in 7.21, 24, 28 or the
eighteen occurrences of 'by faith' in 11.1–40.

(iv) Alliteration

This is another type of repetition, this time of the sounds of letter or syl-
lables. The sermon begins with a striking and effective instance of this
feature. Of the twelve Greek words in 1.1, three of the first four and two
of the last four begin with a 'p', and the first phrase is particularly
sonorous through its further repetition of the 'l' sound (in transliteration
polumerōs: kai polutropōs palai).

(v) Inclusio

This is yet a further type of repetition, which entails reproducing at the
end of a unit a term or terms used at the beginning. So, to take just one
example, in 6.13–7.28 there is mention, toward the beginning, of God's
swearing (6.13), God's oath (6.16) and Jesus as a high priest for ever
(6.20), while at the end of the section there is a return to this language of
God's swearing and oath (7.21, 28) and of a high priest who is a Son for
ever (7.28).

(vi) Chiasm

This arrangement heightens the style by reversing the order in parallel
clauses to produce the pattern represented by ABB'A' where A' and B'
refer to the same or similar words or thoughts as in the content of clauses
A and B. The pattern can be found in simple and more elaborate forms.

In 4.16 the order of the Greek words is 'receive mercy and grace find' so that the first verb and noun correspond to the second noun and verb in chiastic fashion. In the same context the pattern is found on a somewhat larger scale with themes, so that 2.17 introduces Jesus as a merciful and faithful high priest and in what follows the order of the descriptive adjectives is reversed, the quality of faithfulness being treated first (cf. 3.1–6) and then the quality of mercy (cf. 4.14–5.10).

(vii) Exempla

The use of fitting examples was another common technique practised by effective orators. A prime instance in Hebrews is the sequence of brief portraits of figures from Israel's history in 11.4–40, who exemplify the enduring faith called for in 10.19–39 and described in 11.1, 2.

(viii) Hyperbole

Overstatement for effect was another frequent feature of powerful rhetoric. The assertion that certain people are crucifying again the Son of God (6.6) is clearly not a literal possibility but achieves maximum rhetorical impact in suggesting how unthinkable the rejection of Christ and his benefits should be. Once such use of rhetoric is observed, questions may arise about other language in the same context. Is the statement in 6.4 that it is impossible to repent after falling away an exaggeration designed to put the perils that face the readers in the strongest possible terms? Or is the assertion that follows in 6.9, designed to gain the goodwill of the addressees – 'we are confident of better things in your case' – also hyperbole? If the writer were really confident, would he be writing to issue such a warning in the first place?

Present-day readers can be confident that, with its incorporation of such a range of rhetorical devices, Hebrews would have been recognized by its original audience, whatever their response, as the skilful composition of an experienced preacher.

The preacher's rhetoric: a summary

Clearly Hebrews is not the sort of sermon that has been produced on the spur of the moment. Its preacher has felt his way into the problems and discouragements his hearers are facing, reflected on them deeply as he pondered the Scriptures, and been given the insights to make connections with their situation. In the process his sermon becomes the vehicle for God's earlier word, as it is read in the light of reflection on the significance of what God has now done in Christ, speaking again to the hearers. But that is not all. The preacher has clearly worked hard at crafting the sermon, choosing what will be the most effective language and employing all the rhetorical skills at his disposal to ensure that its argument will convince, that it will capture both his hearers' minds and their emotions, and that it will press home his message with urgency and compassion. Seen in this way, it can be said to contain features that make it an excellent model for any preacher. What is more, it reflects a confidence about the efficacy of preaching. Faced with a community that is in danger of drifting and finding other options more attractive than its confession of faith, this pastor does not suggest superficial remedies. Instead he preaches, and he preaches Scripturally, theologically and Christologically in a sermon which is directly targeted at the most pressing basic needs of the hearers and which does not shrink from confronting these boldly.

Further reading

On genre issues, see D. E. Aune (1987) *The New Testament in Its Literary Environment* (Philadelphia: Westminster), pp. 197–214; Trotter 1997: 59–80.

On the rhetorical dimensions of Hebrews, see the following:

J. Swetnam (1969) 'On the Literary Genre of the "Epistle" to the Hebrews', *NovTest* 11, pp. 261–69.

L. Wills (1984) 'The form of the sermon in Hellenistic Judaism and early Christianity', *HTR* 77, pp. 277–99.

C. C. Black (1988) 'The Rhetorical form of the Hellenistic Jewish and early Christian sermon: a response to Lawrence Wills', *HTR* 81, pp. 1–18.

C. F. Evans (1988) 'The Theology of Rhetoric: The Epistle to the Hebrews' Friends of Dr. Williams' Library, Lecture 42; London: Dr. Williams' Trust.

B. Lindars (1989) 'The Rhetorical Structure of Hebrews', *NTS* 35, pp. 382–406.

T. H. Olbricht (1993) 'Hebrews as Amplification' in S. E. Porter and T. H. Olbricht (eds), *Rhetoric and the New Testament: Essays from the 1992 Heidelberg Conference. JSNTSup*90. Sheffield: Sheffield Academic Press, pp. 375–87.

On the phenomenon of midrash, see G. G. Porton, 'Midrash' in D. N. Freedman (ed.), *The Anchor Bible Dictionary*, Vol. 3 (New York: Doubleday, 1992), pp. 818–22.

On issues surrounding the final chapter, see most recently A. J. M. Wedderburn (2004) 'The "Letter" to the Hebrews and its Thirteenth Chapter', *NTS* 50, pp. 390–405.

3

The Structure of the Argument

An outline of the main divisions of Hebrews

Outlines of the argument of Hebrews are notoriously difficult to construct, and hardly any two scholars agree on the details. This is partly because commentators and others are using different criteria for constructing their outlines. In broad terms, one can distinguish those who operate primarily in terms of content from those who focus more on linguistic and semantic analysis, paying attention to formal features, to links and transitions signalled by the text's language. The former tend to divide up the epistle topically, often with headings about Christ's superiority, and there is nothing wrong with that type of analysis. Nevertheless, such headings inevitably simplify the content of the sections, failing to do justice to the variety of the material in them and to the way in which sections can in fact overlap in their treatment of themes and development of the argument.

One of the features of Hebrews that makes life difficult for those who like structured schemes and diagrammatic outlines is that, after stating a theme and then developing it, its author can then, for clearly thought out reasons, digress to another related topic, but then return skilfully to the original theme, while managing to incorporate elements of the digression into the further development of that theme. Students intent on discovering the structure by following every detailed twist and turn of the argument and its linguistic connections can end up with horrendously detailed and complex outlines for the epistle. In addition, as soon as they provide any titles or headings for their divisions other than the precise words of the text, they too are involved in decisions about content that inevitably move them somewhat in the direction of a topical treatment.

After becoming aware of the difficulties and the lack of agreement among scholars, one might well wonder why they bother. What is the point of an outline anyway? An outline functions as an initial map offered by a more experienced reader to enable other readers to negotiate the unfamiliar terrain of a text's argument. Provided that it is recognized that it has only this limited value, that it makes no strong claims to having been the design in the original author's mind, and that it acknowledges its provisionality and need for modification and expansion as readers make their own discoveries, then the attempt to produce one may be a useful exercise. The most helpful outline is likely to be one that attempts to combine the most salient features of both form and content and, in the case of Hebrews, does some justice, without becoming over-elaborate, to its extended treatment of Scriptural passages, to its intercalation of exposition and paraenesis, and to major overlaps of material.

What follows builds on the earlier discussion of genre and rhetoric in its suggested outline, and the sketch of the argument that is then provided puts some flesh on the skeleton and clarifies why the argument is seen as progressing in this particular way.

A. The written sermon (1.1–12.29)

1. Introduction: God's speech in the Son (1.1–4) – exordium

2. Main argument (1.5–12.17) – argumentatio

(i) Exhortation based on Superiority of the Son to Mediators of Old Covenant (1.5–4.13)

    a) Superiority of exalted Christ as Son to angels (1.5–2.4) [with catena of Scriptural texts] and concluding with Exhortation to pay heed to the message of God's salvation in 2.1–4

    b) Christ as representative of humanity made lower than the angels to deal with death (2.5–18) [Exposition of Ps. 8.5–7]

    c) Superiority of Christ as Son to Moses (3.1–6)

    d) Exhortation to enter rest in contrast to Israelites under Moses and Joshua (3.7–4.13) [Exposition of Ps. 95.7–11 with Num. 14.1–35 and Gen. 2.2]

(ii) Exhortation based on Superiority of Christ's High Priesthood to that of Old Covenant (4.14–10.39)

    a) Christ's qualifications to be the Son who is high priest (4.14–5.10) introduced by

Transitional Exhortation in 4.14–16 to hold fast to confession of
Jesus as Son and high priest

b) Exhortation to persevere and progress in order to understand
about Christ's high priesthood (5.11–6.12)

c) God's oath and Christ's Melchizedek priesthood (6.13–7.28)
[with treatment of Ps. 110.4 and Gen. 14.17–20]

d) Superiority of Christ's high priesthood to arrangements under the
Aaronic priesthood (8.1–10.18)
(i) Christ's heavenly high priesthood and mediation of the new
covenant (8.1–13)
[with use of Jer. 31.31–34]
(ii) Christ's heavenly high priesthood and his final once-for-all
sacrifice for sins (9.1–10.18)
[based on Exod. 24–26; Lev. 16, 17 with exposition of Ps. 40.6–8]

e) Exhortation to appropriate and remain true to the salvation
provided through Christ as high priest (10.19–39) concluded by
Transitional Exhortation in 10.32–39 to faith and endurance
[with use of Hab. 2.3, 4 and Isa. 26.20]

(iii) Exhortation to Endurance based on Faith (11.1–12.17)

a) Exposition of faith illustrated by examples from Israel's history
(11.1–40)

b) Exhortation to endurance (12.1–17)
[Exposition of Prov. 3.11, 12]

3. Concluding exhortation based on God's speech from heaven in Christ (12.18–29) – peroratio

Final Exposition of the superiority of the new covenant to the old
(12.18–24), concluding with:
Exhortation not to refuse the one who speaks but to give thanks
(12.25–29)

B. Epistolary conclusion (13.1–25)

1) Various concluding exhortations (13.1–19)
2) Benediction (13.20, 21)
3) Comment on the letter (13.22)
4) News of Timothy and Travel Plans (13.23)
5) Greetings (13.24)
6) Grace benediction (13.25)

The flow of the argument

The first four verses (1.1–4) provide an extremely effective introduction to this written homily. With the use of traditional material in 1.2b, 3 they remind the readers of the exalted status of Christ as God's Son both in relation to the cosmos and to God. At the same time the introduction sets up the series of comparisons that will dominate what follows. It opens with the comparison between God's speaking in former times and God's speaking in the last days, and closes with a comparison of Christ to the angels. There are other key elements that will be developed as the argument progresses – the notion of God speaking in the Son, the depiction of Christ's accomplishment in cultic and sacrificial terms as making purification for sins, and the portrayal of his present status, in terms of Ps. 110.1, as being seated at the right hand of God.

The homily then moves straight into its main argument (1.5–12.17) and this will develop in three parts. The first (1.5–4.13) will treat God's word in Christ as Son, picking up this designation from the introduction. The second (4.14–10.39) will treat Christ as high priest, a role implied by the introduction's talk of his making purification for sin. In this role Christ will also be seen as an embodiment of God's speech or word, this time specifically God's oath. The third part (11.1–12.17) will expand on the readers' need for faith and endurance, already mentioned more briefly several times in the sermon, not least in the transitional last part of the previous section.

Taking off from the first statement of the prologue about the revelation of God in Christ in comparison with that of the past, the first main part of the sermon's argument (1.5–4.13) develops the comparison in terms of the superiority of the revelation in Christ as Son to that through the mediators of the old covenant. Through the characteristic technique of employing hook words, 1.5–2.4 picks up on the comparison with angels who were introduced in 1.4. By juxtaposing a number of Scriptural texts, the writer shows that what is said of the Son in contrast to what is said of angels makes the former far superior. The comparison with angels is neither an anomaly in this opening section, nor discussed primarily because the readers had some problem with their view of angels. As 2.2 makes clear, the angels are treated because of their association with the giving of the law and therefore seen as mediators of the revelation under the old covenant. In the exhortation that concludes this section in 2.1–4 the comparison between the message declared by angels and the message of salvation that has come to the readers is the basis for a warning about the consequences of not heeding or of drifting away from the latter message.

In 2.5–18 the comparison with the angels is given a new twist, as, reflecting on Ps. 8, the writer sees Jesus as having been made lower than the angels for a while in order that, as the representative human, he should be able to deal with death. In solidarity with his human brothers and sisters Jesus pioneered the path to glory through suffering and, in the process, rescued them from the power of death. This identification with humanity and its suffering also qualified Jesus to be a merciful and faithful high priest and one who would be able to represent humans in sacrificing for them. Here the key theme that will be treated in the extensive middle section of the argument from 4.14–10.39 is already anticipated.

Before that, however, the notion of Jesus' faithfulness, particularly as God's Son, is elaborated in 3.1–6 in comparison with Moses. Under the old covenant Moses was indeed faithful in God's house as a servant, but Christ is depicted as faithful over God's house as a son. The comparison ends with the assertion that Christian believers are God's house, God's people, if they maintain their commitment.

This assertion leads, in 3.7–4.13, to a direct exhortation to the readers, based on Ps. 95.7–11, not to turn away from the living God by hardening their hearts in unbelief and disobedience. They are not to be like the wilderness generation who missed out, through unbelief, on the rest that God had prepared for them. The wilderness generation fell by the sword (cf. Num. 14.42, 43) but the readers face the still more penetrating judgement of the word of God that is sharper than any two-edged sword. This mention of God's word provides an *inclusio* with the introduction and the opening of this section (cf. 1.1, 2; 2.1–4).

Having given his warning, the writer moves to the central part of his argument about Jesus as high priest and his superiority to the priesthood of the old covenant (4.14–10.39). This extended middle section of the sermon's tripartite main argument is introduced and concluded by transitional hortatory passages (4.14–16; 10.32–39), showing its overlapping connections with what precedes and what follows and demonstrating the writer's skill in sustaining continuity of thought. The exhortation to the recipients in 4.14–16 to hold fast their confession and approach God's throne with boldness in order to receive grace is based on a depiction of Jesus as Son and high priest that takes up the qualities that he was said to have in 2.17, 18, namely, his having experienced testing as the Son in such a way that he is able to be a merciful high priest. The qualifications for these roles are expanded on in 5.1–10. Like the Aaronic priesthood, Christ was chosen through God's call. He was appointed as Son in the words of Ps. 2.7 and appointed as high priest after the order of Melchizedek in the words of Ps. 110.4. As the Son, in his facing of death, he learned the obedience that enabled him to be perfected to become the source of an eternal salvation as the high priest for ever according to the order of Melchizedek.

At this point the writer senses that his continued elaboration of this theme may tax his readers' understanding. In 5.11–6.12, therefore, he digresses temporarily to admonish them for not having reached the necessary level of maturity in their discernment of such matters, urging them to move on with him from basic teachings about Christ. This will occur if God permits it. But here he issues a strong warning that, in the case of those who have been enlightened and have then fallen away, who have in effect crucified the son of God again, it will be impossible for them to be restored. In the next breath, however, he hastens to reassure his readers that he does not envisage such a fate in their case, but that nevertheless they must abandon their sluggishness, rekindle the enthusiasm they once showed, and exercise faith and endurance if they are to attain confident assurance of inheriting God's promises.

The writer can now return, in 6.13–7.28, to his argument about Jesus as high priest according to the order of Melchizedek. But, using 'promise' as his hook word and with some deference to his audience's dullness of understanding, he does not immediately take up the previous thread by treating Melchizedek's priesthood itself but leads up to this by first discussing God's swearing of a promise to Abraham. He underlines that God's promise confirmed by an oath guarantees its fulfilment and that this ought to be a source of encouragement to the readers, as heirs of such a promise, to seize hold on its assured hope. In fact, they now have that hope securely embodied in Jesus and anchored in heaven, since he has entered the inner sanctum of the heavenly tabernacle on their behalf as a high priest for ever according to the order of Melchizedek. With reference to the narrative in Gen. 14, the writer shows how this passage allows Melchizedek to be seen as a priest for ever and as thus resembling the Son of God and how it depicts him as superior to Abraham, since he received tithes from Abraham and blessed him. Such a depiction enables him to make the further point that, since Abraham was the ancestor of Levi, Abraham in his action represented Levi, and thus the levitical priesthood, which can be seen as an inferior mortal priesthood paying tithes to the priest who lives for ever.

This portrayal, together with talk in Ps. 110 of another priest according to the order of Melchizedek, signals that perfection was not achievable by means of the levitical priesthood and that a change would be necessary both in the priesthood and in the law that accompanied it. The necessity for change is all the more evident when it is remembered that Christ was descended from Judah and not Levi. This requires an ineffectual law about physical descent to be set aside in favour of the introduction of a better hope represented by the one who has become priest according to the power of his indestructible life, the one whom Ps. 110.4 designates as a priest for ever according to the order of Melchizedek. What is more, the oath by which this priest is appointed, according to the psalm, makes Jesus the guarantee of a better covenant.

The writer then stresses the advantages of the priesthood under the better covenant. Whereas the levitical priests, because of their mortality, were continually changing, Christ's priesthood is for ever and he always lives to save and intercede for those who approach God through him. While high priests under the law had continually to offer sacrifices both for themselves and for the people, Christ, as the holy and exalted high priest, was able to offer himself once for all. Finally, whereas the law appointed high priests who were subject to weakness, the word of the oath appoints a Son who has been perfected for ever.

As a good preacher and teacher, the writer pauses, after what has been an intricate argument involving the Melchizedek priesthood, to remind his audience of his main point, before proceeding to expound in two further ways (8.1–13 and 9.1–10.18) on the superiority of Christ's high priesthood to the arrangements under the Aaronic priesthood. He sums up his key theme in terms of believers having the perfected Son as high priest, who is seated at God's right hand and ministers in the true heavenly tabernacle set up by God. From this perspective it is now argued in this first subsection (8.1–13), which takes up the language of 5.1, where the comparison with the Aaronic priesthood was already anticipated, that the priests who offer sacrifices according to the law do so in a sanctuary that is only a shadow of the true heavenly one. By entering heaven, therefore, Jesus has a superior ministry and so is also the mediator of a better covenant established through better promises. After all, there would have been no need for the promise of a second covenant if there had been no fault with the first. But the promise of a new covenant in Jer. 31.31–34 is seen as indicating that the arrangements under the first one were deficient and that with the arrival of the new the first becomes obsolete.

The second sub-section (9.1–10.18) begins by describing the basic arrangements in what the writer calls the earthly or first tabernacle, and focuses on its outer and inner sections. In particular, he sees in the limited access to the inner sanctuary of only the high priest, and then only once a year, an indication that proper access still awaits and that the blood that is offered there is able to deal only with external physical matters and is ineffective in relation to the worshipper's conscience. In contrast Christ, as the high priest of the eschatological realities, entered into the heavenly holy place once for all and not with animal blood but with his own blood. The quality of Christ's blood offering, since it is made through the eternal spirit, produces an eternal redemption in which the conscience is cleansed. In this way Christ is the mediator of a better covenant, enabling believers to receive the promised inheritance. What was decisive was his death that redeemed them from the sins committed under the first covenant. In a play on the term 'covenant', which can also mean 'testament' or 'will', the writer makes the point that, for a will to come into effect, the death of the testator must be established. Indeed there had to be death when the first covenant was inaugurated, and the blood of the calves and goats that were killed was sprinkled on the law scroll, the people, the tabernacle and its vessels. In comparison with these arrangements, Christ entered heaven itself, not a merely human representation of it, and he did not make a repeated offering of blood that was not his own but he appeared once for all and dealt with sin by the sacrifice of himself. The law is only a shadow of the eschatological realities and its continual sacrifices are unable to perfect worshippers or to take away sins. In contrast, Christ can be seen as taking up the words of Ps. 40. He says, 'Sacrifices and offerings you have not desired, but a body you have prepared for me' and 'see, I have come to do your will'. Thereby he abolishes the law's offerings and establishes God's will through the offering of his own body once for all. And whereas under the old arrangements priests stood day after day to offer their ineffectual sacrifices, Christ, having offered his one sacrifice for all time, sat down at God's right hand. The perfection he accomplished for humans by that one sacrifice includes the forgiveness of sins promised in the new covenant and means that there is no further need for any sin offering.

Now that his comparison of the new covenant situation of Christ's high priesthood with the old covenant arrangements for the Aaronic priests has been completed, the writer can engage in an extended exhortation on the basis of his conclusions (10.19–39). Since by his death their great high priest has opened up a new and living way into the heavenly sanctuary, believers should worship with full assurance of faith and with cleansed hearts and bodies, should hold fast to their confession, and should not neglect to meet together but instead encourage one another. However, for those who wilfully persist in sin after receiving knowledge of the truth no further sacrifice is available, only fiery judgement. If the person who violated the Mosaic law had to die, then the punishment for the one who profanes the blood of the new covenant will be much worse. But the readers are then urged instead to recall earlier times when they did endure suffering and persecution, showed solidarity with their fellow sufferers and accepted the plundering of their possessions, knowing they possessed something more lasting than earthly goods. If they are to receive what has been promised, they have need of the same quality of endurance now. Using a combination of Hab. 2.3, 4 and Isa. 26.20, whose wording, as we have noted earlier, also forms an *inclusio* with that of Ps. 40.6–8, the writer encourages and admonishes them with the divine assertion that the coming one will come shortly, that in the meantime the righteous person is to live by faith, and that God takes no pleasure in the person who shrinks back. Aligning himself with the readers, the writer claims that he and they are not among those who shrink back and are lost, but among those who have faith and are saved. In this way the last part of this exhortation – 10.32–39 – stresses the need for endurance based on faith and serves as a transition into the final section of the main argument, which will treat this topic more fully and deal with these two qualities, endurance and faith, but in the reverse order.

The writer begins his exposition about faith by defining it in relation to both temporal and spatial categories. In regard to the former, it is the assurance of what is hoped for, and, in regard to the latter, it is the conviction about unseen realities. The formulation 'by faith' then runs throughout this section (11.1–40), connecting the various examples provided by the list of the heroes and heroines selected for treatment. They consist first of characters from the primeval era, then of Abraham and the patriarchs, with most space being devoted to Abraham, and then Moses and the Israelites, but also including Rahab, with most space being devoted to Moses. The depictions of these figures are adapted to the situation of the addressees by highlighting their facing of persecution, abuse and death. This emphasis continues in the summary mention of and allusions to figures from the period of the judges through the time of the prophets down to the time of the Maccabean martyrs. Interspersed with these depictions are comments on the significance of various aspects of faith and particularly on the relation of the faith exercised to the actual fulfilment of the promises. It is this that is stressed at the end of the list, where an *inclusio* is provided with the beginning through the language of receiving testimony and where the writer asserts that, despite their faith, these heroes and heroines did not receive what was promised. God had planned for something better, the inauguration of which brings the perfecting of faith both for those earlier figures and for those who at the present time believe in Christ.

The first verses of chapter 12 are sometimes included in the preceding unit with some wavering over whether 12.1, 2 or 12.1–3 should be included. There is indeed some overlap here between sections, which is not surprising, since faith and endurance are closely related qualities. But the *inclusio* noted above indicates that 11.1–40 should be seen as a unit complete in itself. In addition, in the first few verses of chapter 12 there is not a direct move from Israel's examples of faith to Jesus as the culminating example. Rather the immediate shift of focus is now onto believers who have something better than those who went before them. In taking up the challenge, they indeed look to Jesus as the pioneer and perfecter of faith, yet it is his endurance that is emphasized as an example, and it is to endurance, the main topic in what follows, rather than faith itself, that the readers are exhorted. This exhortation begins by picturing the mass of witnesses from the preceding section to be now functioning as spectators, so that the readers can be urged to run their race with endurance, as they focus their attention on the endurance of the one who has brought faith to completion and pioneered the way ahead. Unlike him, they have not yet had to shed their blood and should endure the trials they do have to face in the light of Prov. 3.11, 12 and in the confidence that this indicates that they are God's legitimate children whom God is training through discipline. In line with the athletic imagery of training for the race, they are not to allow themselves to become flabby but to strengthen their limbs and make sure they run a race that takes them straight to the goal. This goal can be depicted in terms of communal peace and holiness, and it is in this context that there follows a warning to watch out that no one in the community allow bitterness to fester and to taint others. They are to be vigilant lest anyone become like Esau, who was willing to sell his inheritance for the sake of immediate gratification. And in line with his previous warnings against apostasy, the writer points out that Esau had no second chance to repent and regain what he had forfeited.

The writer now brings his homily to a climax in 12.18–29 with a final comparison between revelation under the old covenant and revelation under the new. The passage contains the type of features one would expect of a discourse's *peroratio*, particularly the recapitulation of leading themes, which drive home the key message for a last time in a heightened emotional appeal to the audience. It paints a graphic picture intended to arouse fear and gratitude. It also provides an *inclusio* with the first part of the homily in 1.1–2.4, with its return to the comparison of God's speaking in the past and in the present, and the exhortation to heed based on that comparison. It takes up the mention of angels who are now worshippers in the new covenant situation rather than associated with the old. It also returns to the notion that the earth and the heavens will perish whereas God remains, and now associates believers with that which remains. The *peroratio* first pictures the scene of the giving of the old covenant at Sinai, and does so in such a way as to stress its physical and tangible aspects and to evoke dread. Then, in contrast, believers are said to have come in their worship to the invisible heavenly realities. Those assembled at the heavenly Zion consist of the living God as judge, innumerable angels, the firstborn (all those who share the inheritance of the first born par excellence, cf. 1.6), the perfected spirits of the righteous, and Jesus, the new covenant mediator, with his sprinkled blood that speaks eloquently of grace. The exhortation based on the contrasting earthly and heavenly scenes urges the addressees not to refuse the one who is now speaking in Christ. If those who refused the one who warned them on earth did not escape judgement, how much less able to escape will those be who refuse the one who warns them from heaven and who will shake the created heaven and earth. But what believers will receive is that which remains, an unshakeable kingdom, and that prospect should induce the gratitude that motivates acceptable worship. This worship will also be accompanied by reverence and awe, since the living God is not only gracious but also a consuming fire.

Having completed his homily with a rhetorical flourish the writer continues his written form of communication in the more usual fashion, with the whole of chapter 13 now taking up the elements that would be found at the end of an epistolary communication. There is no longer the same sustained rhetoric that has characterized what has preceded, but there is enough about the contents to indicate that they are integrated with what has come before in the homily proper and do not form a separate section which was added on at a later time.

First, there are various concluding exhortations about mutual love, hospitality to strangers, remembering those in prison, marriage, love of money, remembering former leaders, strange teachings, offering sacrifices of praise, good deeds and sharing, and submitting to present leaders. In the context of the warning against strange teachings the writer makes one last comparison of the old and the new. If these teachings are a reference to the sacrificial significance being attached by some to Jewish meals, the writer declares that, in contrast, Christian believers have their own altar. Using Lev. 16.27, 28, he recalls the practice of the bodies of sacrificial animals, whose blood was brought into the sanctuary, having to be burned outside the camp. Such a practice enables an analogy to be made with Jesus' sacrificial death, which took place outside the city gate of Jerusalem in order to sanctify the people. The analogy leads into an appeal to the readers to go to Jesus outside the camp, outside the Jewish religious system, in order there to bear the shame he endured. This would be a move that is in line with the conviction that in this world believers have no lasting city but seek the city that is to come.

After these various exhortations, the writer asks for prayer for himself and his associates, particularly that he might be restored to the company of his readers. There follows a benediction, which refers to Jesus as the great shepherd of the sheep and mentions the blood of the eternal covenant, which has as its prayer wish the notion that God may equip the readers to do what is pleasing in God's sight, and which closes in a doxology. Next, the comment on the letter exhorts the readers to bear with its exhortation! News of Timothy and the writer's plans, greetings, and a final grace benediction round off the epistle.

Further reading

See the monographs of Vanhoye 1989 and Guthrie 1994 and the shorter orientation to some of the issues in S. Stanley (1994) 'The Structure of Hebrews from Three Perspectives [Genre, Rhetoric, Content]', *Tyndale Bulletin* 45, pp. 245–71.

4

Background Issues

The issues surrounding authorship, recipients and date of Hebrews are well rehearsed in the introductions to commentaries on Hebrews and in more general New Testament Introductions. For this reason and because, in any case, there is little hard evidence beyond the minimal textual data on which to base any conclusions, treatment of them will form only the first part of this chapter, the rest of which will be devoted to surveying the possible backgrounds of thought against which Hebrews as a first-century document may be best understood.

Authorship

The discussion of this topic can be summed up by asking, 'If not Paul, who?' and by then answering (echoing Origen), 'God only knows'. As has already been indicated, the anonymity of Hebrews plagued the history of its acceptance as canonical at a time when the church was looking to confirm the apostolicity of the content of its authoritative texts by associating them with particular figures from the apostolic era. Despite Hebrews achieving canonical status through its association with Paul, we can be virtually certain that Paul was not its author. Its canonical history already points to this conclusion. As noted in our first chapter, Hebrews was used in the early second century in Rome but not attributed to Paul when alluded to or cited. It then fell into relative disuse and doubts were raised about its stance on post-baptismal repentance. Only later towards the end of the fourth century, under the influence of its attribution to Paul in the eastern church, did a cautious consensus emerge that it was to be included in the Pauline letter collection. The history of its reception in the West would have been a very different story if there had been any clear tradition tying Hebrews to the apostle Paul. Paul's personal stamp is all over his letters. It is difficult to imagine his writing one which does not mention his apostolic authority and in which he remains anonymous and does not allow either his personality or his distinctive conception of the gospel to emerge. He would scarcely have described his relation to the message of salvation as one in which he simply places himself among those to whom it was attested by those who heard the Lord (2.3). Whereas Christ's resurrection is of pivotal significance in Paul's thought, Hebrews stresses instead Christ's exaltation and mentions his resurrection explicitly only in the closing benediction (cf. 13.20). Paul does mention the intercession of the exalted Christ for believers (Rom. 8.34) but any explicit mention of Christ as the heavenly high priest, which is Hebrews' central Christological image, is entirely missing from the Pauline Corpus.

If the author was not Paul, then the most likely candidate appears to have been someone in the Pauline circle of associates or known to the Pauline churches, since 13.23 mentions 'our brother, Timothy' as an associate of the writer and as someone who is known to the recipients. Given recent attempts to recover the role of women in the early Christian movement, it would be appropriate if that someone were Priscilla. This suggestion has in fact been put forward by A. von Harnack ('Probabilia über die Adresse and den Verfasser des Hebräerbriefes', *ZNW* 1 (1900), pp. 16–41) and was given an extensive treatment by R. Hoppin (*Priscilla, Author of the Epistle to the Hebrews and Other Essays*. New York: Exposition, 1969). But without a further hypothesis about the need for disguising one's gender, which would in any case undermine the likelihood of a woman's authoritative teaching role being readily accepted in a first-century Jewish Christian context, this proposal is ruled out by the use of the masculine form of the participle at 11.32 – 'time would fail me for telling . . . (*diëgoumenon*)'. If one were simply forced to choose a candidate from all the figures in the first generation of Christians known to us in early Christian literature, and thereby to arrogate to oneself the knowledge Origen sensibly left to the deity, then, despite his ambivalent stance toward the contents of the letter, Luther's guess, in a sermon published in 1522, is as good as any and might even turn out to be an inspired one. He opted for an associate of both Paul and Priscilla, namely Apollos, who, according to Acts 18.24–28, was a Hellenistic Jewish Christian, originating from Alexandria, rhetorically effective in his teaching, and able to help fellow believers because his profound knowledge of Scripture was instrumental in enabling them to see from the sacred texts that Jesus was the Messiah. But considerations of dating also enter the picture here. If, for whatever reason, one is inclined to date Hebrews after 70 CE, then the later the dating the less likely that Apollos or other acquaintances of Paul would still have been alive. Timothy, whom the tradition portrays as a very young associate, could plausibly have still been exercising an active ministry until the mid-80s and been available for mention by the writer until that date.

But the anonymity of Hebrews is a prime instance of what is true of much of the New Testament, with the exception of the undisputed letters of Paul, that is, that we know virtually nothing about the actual authors. Interpretation is, therefore, primarily dependent on the documents themselves and what we can discover about their likely general cultural context. In the case of authorship, this means having to be content with the documents' implied authors whom we attempt to reconstruct from clues within the text. Whatever theoretical stance might be taken on the question of the importance of knowledge of an author and that author's intent, the benefits that have been derived from the reading of Hebrews within the church in the absence of such knowledge indicate that in practice at least it proves to be by no means essential.

Recipients

Most of our useful knowledge about the recipients of Hebrews also comes from picking up on the clues that the text provides about their situation and experiences. When the move is made from such implied readers, who will be treated more fully under Occasion and Purposes, to attempting to specify more concretely the actual Christians to whom Hebrews was sent, two major issues emerge: their ethnic identity and their location.

The most likely initial impression of present-day readers is that the original recipients would have needed an intimate knowledge of the Jewish Scriptures and the details of the cultic arrangements within Judaism in order to appreciate its message, and that therefore these addressees would have been Jewish Christians. The impression may turn out to be basically correct, but it is one likely to have also been informed by the title this document has in the New Testament. As has been noted, however, the superscription, 'to the Hebrews', was in all probability added later by a scribe or editor, who was seeking an analogous title for this letter to those of Paul's letters, which were given titles in relation to their addressees. The title supplied in this case would also have been an inference from the contents of the text. Once this is realized, then there are at least grounds for re-examining the common assumption about the ethnic background of the recipients. Indeed scholars have from time to time proposed that the title is entirely misleading and that the recipients of this document were in fact Gentile Christians.

How could this be, given that the contents of Hebrews are so clearly dominated by themes central to Judaism, and that the thrust of the argument is to demonstrate the superiority of the new covenant inaugurated in Christ? In response, it is argued that these themes and the theological argument are not necessarily directly related to the situation of the addressees and that in the paraenetical sections of the letter there are no explicit warnings about going back to Judaism but rather general exhortations to endure in the face of opposition and not to become discouraged or to apostasize. Such exhortations, it is claimed, could be addressed to Gentile Christians, and the theological arguments about the superiority to Judaism are simply to be read as underlining the finality and absoluteness of the Christian message and therefore the seriousness of drifting away from it. It is also suggested that some of the formulations the author employs appear to be directed to Gentiles rather than Jews. In 6.1, for example, he talks of the foundational teaching the readers had received and lists among its topics 'repentance from dead works and faith toward God, instruction about baptisms, laying on of hands, resurrection of the dead, and eternal judgment', matters in which those from a pagan background rather than Jews would have needed instruction. Likewise, it is suggested, having 'an evil unbelieving heart that turns away from the living God' (3.12) is too strong an indictment of Christians returning to their Jewish beliefs, and better fits Gentiles going back to paganism. None of these arguments is particularly compelling. The negative comments on Judaism within the theological exposition do give the impression that Judaism is in some way an immediate threat to the sense of their identity that the writer is attempting to encourage in the recipients. Even if the elementary teachings the writer mentions had their background in Judaism, as seems likely, it is also clear that they would be given distinctive content within Christian catechesis, and for the writer 'the living God' is precisely the God who has been shown to be alive in the divine speaking and acting in Jesus Christ so that any response, whether by Jew or Gentile, which did not do sufficient justice to such an understanding would be a turning away from this living God.

A more plausible case that the recipients were Gentile Christians can be made if they are viewed as those who had been God-fearers, sympathetic adherents of the synagogue, and who had then converted to the Christian movement but were now experiencing doubts and, under the threat of persecution, were again feeling the attractions of the religion that had elicited their sympathy in the first place and that offered more political legitimacy and protection. Such Gentile 'Judaizers' are known to us from other literature around the end of the first century and beginning of the second, namely, the epistle of Barnabas and the letters of Ignatius. But this depiction of the addressees places them in substantially the same position as the more traditional view assigns to Jewish Christian readers, and there are no clear grounds for departing from tradition here. The intricate knowledge of the Scriptures which the writer assumes in the readers, while by no means impossible in the case of Gentile God-fearers, more naturally favours the view that they were Jewish Christians, as do the direct assertions and exhortations to the readers in 13.9–13, culminating in their being urged to go to Jesus 'outside the camp', i.e. outside the Jewish religious system, and to bear the abuse this would entail. Whoever formulated the title for this letter is likely to have drawn the appropriate inference: the Christians addressed were primarily Jewish in their background, although that there were among them some Gentile former God-fearers, who were facing the same issues, cannot be ruled out.

The issue of the location of the readers initially revolves around the interpretation of 13.24b – 'those from Italy send you greetings'. Does the reference to Italy reflect the fact that the writer is in Italy and is sending greetings from Italian believers to a community elsewhere in the empire? Or does it mean that he is writing from outside Italy and is sending greetings to a Christian community in Italy from some of their Christian compatriots who happen to be in the same location as he is? The second option is far more likely. It makes much better sense that a writer elsewhere would single out for special mention among his companions those who were compatriots of the recipients than that someone writing from within Italy would include greetings from all believers across Italy. This obviates the need for any treatment of other suggestions for the readers' location, among which have been Jerusalem and Colossae and for which there is even less clear evidence from the letter or its reception history. If the recipients were most likely to be a group of Christians in Italy, then the scholarly proposal (dating back at least to the middle of the eighteenth century) that the epistle was sent to Rome provides the best option for their location in Italy. There were Christians elsewhere in the country but a Roman location best fits the bill for a place where the gospel was first preached by eyewitnesses (cf. 2.3) and where, as the content of the letter implies, there had at the very least been a significant Jewish Christian heritage. It also fits the facts that Timothy was known to Christians in Rome (cf. Rom. 16.21) and that the earliest attestation of the epistle comes from Rome (cf. *1 Clement* and The Shepherd of Hermas).

How well would a setting in Rome match the reference in 10.32–34 to a wave of persecution endured by the recipients in the early days of their Christian experience? This might plausibly refer to what happened when Jewish Christians were expelled from Rome under Claudius around 49 CE. In particular, the plundering of their property is an occurrence likely to befall those who had been forced to leave their homes. If 'the earlier days' after their enlightenment refer to the experience of second-generation Roman Christians, then, of course, the Neronian persecutions in 64–68 CE would provide an even more likely setting. And if, as some hold, the reference to the outcome of former leaders' faith in 13.7 is to be interpreted as their martyrdom, then the deaths of Peter and Paul in Rome at that time could also be in view. The depiction of persecution in

10.32–34, however, fails to mention any deaths, perhaps because its focus is on the experience of the readers who have survived.

One further aspect of the readers' location should be mentioned. There are indications that they were part of a house church within a larger Christian community in that location. While in 13.17 they are exhorted to obey and submit to their leaders, the final exhortation in 13.24 – 'Greet all your leaders and all the saints' – may well suggest that the recipients of this epistle belong to a more extended group, which has leaders and members other than just those who gather in their own particular assemblies. Again this would correspond to what is known about the Christian movement in a large city such as Rome, where there had also been a considerable number of Jewish Christians who were likely to meet together in their own house churches (cf. Rom. 16).

Date

The question of the dating of Hebrews has already arisen in the discussion above, because inevitably it overlaps with some of the matters relevant to authorship and recipients. In comparison with these other two issues, that of dating is more hotly contested and, arguably, more interesting in terms of assessing the evidence within the text and more pertinent to its interpretation. This is because a decision on the matter involves examining whether the author's treatment of the invalidity of the sacrificial system and its priesthood now that Christ has died and been exalted to heaven is in any way a response to the crisis in Judaism that arose from the destruction of the temple in 70 CE. The problem, of course, is that Hebrews' argument does not even mention the temple, let alone its destruction, and is carried out on the basis of the Scriptural instructions about the tabernacle. Are we to assume that this latter phenomenon was part of a common way of discussing the validity of the present temple arrangements, which were taken to be in essential continuity with the earlier regulations about the tabernacle and the sacrificial cult? The assumption appears justified for two reasons. First, the Torah and its liturgical instructions had long been appropriated by the Jerusalem temple. Secondly, it would be very strange if the writer's extensive arguments about the sacrificial system bore no relation to the Judaism with which he and his readers were familiar in their own day.

In this case, does the fact that in some places Hebrews refers to the cultic arrangements in the present tense mean that it is written before their practice was brought to an end by the fate of the Jerusalem temple? But the passages in view, such as 8.4, 5; 9.6, 7; 13.11, are by no means decisive, since they may simply be a graphic way of talking about what held in the past. Perhaps the only text that makes the reader pause is 10.1, 2 which, after stating that under the law the same sacrifices 'are continually offered year after year' and that these are unable to perfect the worshippers, adds 'otherwise, would they not have ceased being offered . . .?' While this is still quite comprehensible after 70 CE as an argument about a past state of affairs, one cannot help asking whether, if the writer were aware of the fact that they had indeed recently ceased, he would have been able to resist pointing this out, since it would appear to offer empirical support for his argument about the provisional nature of the earlier arrangement. On the other hand, this may be to import a modern perspective into the discussion, and, in any case, the force of the argument at this point depends on the contrast between the continuous nature of the old and the once-for-all quality of the new, not on the coming to an end of the old and the arrival of the new. It should also be noted that Josephus (*Ant.* 4.102–87; *C. Ap.* 2.193–98), writing some twenty years after the fall of Jerusalem, can employ the present tense for the offering of sacrifices. If it is objected that Josephus did not believe the temple system had been replaced and that the two cases are therefore not comparable, then one can also point to other Christian writings, which would have had ample cause to refer to the destruction of the temple as part of their discussion but which fail to do so and instead speak as if the sacrificial arrangements were still in place (cf. *1 Clem.* 41.2, 3; *Diogn.* 3.5). Most Jews were likely in fact to have expected the temple to be rebuilt imminently, as it had been after the Babylonian exile. This expectation is reflected in both the choice of the pseudonyms, Ezra and Baruch, for two of the more important apocalypses (cf. *4 Ezra* and *2 Baruch*) and the fact that, as the Mishnah testifies, the rabbis continued to issue rulings about the temple and its sacrifices well after 70 CE.

In this light Hebrews' reference to the tabernacle rather than the temple could be seen as an effective way of undermining any rationale for a rebuilt temple and its cult. As J. D. G. Dunn (*The Partings of the Ways*, London: SCM, 1991, p. 87) puts it, 'it was the very principle of a special cult and special priesthood and continuing sacrifice which the author wished to contest'. The argument from silence about the destruction of the temple cannot therefore be determinative for the dating, and in the end interpreters may have to be content with the less than satisfactory conclusion that Hebrews might have been written at any time between the mid-60s and 90 CE. The *terminus ad quem* is held to be 90 CE, because *1 Clement*, in which references to Hebrews first appear, is usually dated in the mid-90s CE.

Conceptual backgrounds

The author of Hebrews develops his message for the readers by interpreting the Christian gospel about Christ in the light of the Jewish

Scriptures. But neither of these two fundamental factors in his exhortation are unmediated. Both the Jewish Scriptures and the Christian gospel have come to him in a particular first-century context through particular traditions. Our goal here is to survey some of the influential conceptual backgrounds – religious, philosophical and cultural – which might have shaped the creative interaction between Scripture and gospel that distinguishes his homily.

Early Christian tradition

The writer's perspective on Christ is embedded in his early Christian tradition, which already contains interpretation of Jesus' earthly life, his death and exaltation, and his status as God's Son. In 2.3, 4 he insists that the message of salvation is rooted in Jesus' own teaching and the apostolic message – 'confirmed to us by those who heard him'. Most noticeably, he talks about 'the confession' (*homologia*) to indicate the source of the Christology he shares with his addressees. He speaks of 'Jesus, the apostle and high priest of our confession' (3.1) and, after referring to Jesus as high priest and the Son of God, exhorts, 'Let us hold fast to our confession' (4.14) before later repeating, 'Let us hold fast to the confession of our hope' (10.23). In addition, as most scholars hold, 1.2b, 3a right at the outset of the homily take up the language of a confessional formulation. It is also worth noting that Christological confession was already related to and shaped by the Jewish Scriptures in the tradition the writer inherits. So, for example, Ps. 110.1 was already in use to formulate Christ's exaltation as entailing his being seated at the right hand of God. Not only so, but a Christological use of Ps. 8, made in Heb. 2.5–8, is already found in Paul in 1 Cor. 15.25–27, where it is associated with Ps. 110.1. Other contacts with early Christian thought as found in Paul include Hebrews' view of Christ as the pre-existent Son of God (1.2, 3, 6; cf. 1 Cor. 8.6; Phil. 2.5, 6), its notion of his obedience (5.8; cf. Rom. 5.19; Phil. 2.8) and present intercession (7.25; 9.24; cf. Rom. 8.34), its stress on the superiority of the new covenant (8.6–13; cf. 2 Cor. 3.6–11), the play on the meanings 'covenant' and 'testament' (9.15–17; cf. Gal. 3.15–17), its use of Hab. 2.4 in treating faith (10.38; cf. Gal. 3.11; Rom. 1.18), and its comparison between milk and solid food for levels of teaching (5.12–14; cf. 1 Cor. 3.2). In such instances Hebrews is acquainted with the same ideas as Paul but has elaborated them in its own fashion and for its own distinctive purposes.

Some have attempted to be more specific about Hebrews' dependence on earlier Christian tradition. It has, for example, been associated with the figure of Stephen. This view was made popular by W. Manson (*The Epistle to the Hebrews. An Historical and Theological Reconsideration*,

London: Hodder and Stoughton, 1951). He claimed that resemblances between Acts 7 and Hebrews showed that the author of Hebrews stood in the theological tradition of the circle of Stephen and the Hellenistic Jewish Christians, whose views Acts 7 reports. The account of Stephen's speech designates the temple as 'made with hands', a term Hebrews employs for the tabernacle (9.11, 24), and argues that the temple was never intended to become a permanent institution. The speech depicts the people of God as on the move (cf. Heb. 3.7–4.13), has a positive view of the angels as mediators of the law (7.53; cf. Heb. 2.2), speaks of God's word as living (7.38; cf. Heb. 4.12) and of rest in the promised land (7.45, 49; cf. Heb. 4.3). It is difficult to know how to evaluate these connections for two main reasons. First, the speech in Acts is clearly Luke's redaction and the extent and origin of the sources behind it are uncertain. Secondly, Stephen's speech treats the tabernacle favourably and reserves its critique for attitudes to the temple, while Hebrews does not mention the temple but criticizes the tabernacle arrangements as themselves provisional and inadequate in the light of Christ. It is possible, however, that the writer of Hebrews had been familiar with the ideas behind the speech, whatever their exact source, and had taken them in a more radical direction by critiquing the tabernacle foundations of temple worship and drawing more negative conclusions about the implications for the priesthood and the law.

Jewish Scriptures

Hebrews' treatment of the Jewish Scriptures will be dealt with more fully in a later chapter. Here, however, the obvious needs to be stated. Those Scriptures provide the major conceptual framework within which the author interprets the Christian message. They function in Hebrews as an authoritative and effective vehicle of communication for the writer's formulation of his word of exhortation. They provide the point of reference, the language and the symbols the writer and his readers have in common. But Scripture is not treated in a vacuum. The author receives it in its LXX translation and reads it through the lenses of the Jewish exegetical techniques available in the first century. He also receives and interprets it in the context of the development of Jewish thought in the second temple period.

Apocalyptic writings

The main framework for the thought of Hebrews is the developed eschatology, including its cosmology and spatial dualism of heaven and earth, also found in apocalyptic writings, such as *1 Enoch*, *4 Ezra* and *2 Baruch*. A concentration on the heavenly realm and its realities does not require one to posit a more Hellenistic background in Middle Platonism but is already evident in the vertical dimension of the apocalypses familiar within first-century Judaism. What is significant for the interpretation of Hebrews is that in this literature vertical and horizontal dimensions are found side by side, so that a restored Jerusalem and its temple can be depicted both as the heavenly Jerusalem and temple and as the Jerusalem and temple which are to come to earth at the end. Hebrews employs the terminology of the apocalyptic writings about the age to come (6.5) or the world to come (2.5), which was contrasted with this present age. As in the apocalypses, both ages embrace heaven and earth, and the benefits and realities of the future age can be viewed as already anticipated and reserved in the heavenly realm in the present. In early Christianity in general and in Hebrews in particular, what had happened in Christ's death, resurrection and exaltation was seen as the inauguration of the age to come. The present focus of attention for Christian believers now became the heavenly realm to which Christ had been exalted and from which he would return at the consummation of this world's history. Hebrews' primary contribution to this pattern of thought that is derived from the eschatology of the apocalypses is its emphasis on the exalted Christ's role as high priest in the heavenly sanctuary.

Developed views of priesthood and the cult

In elaborating on Christ as high priest, Hebrews is not only dependent on the Pentateuchal materials but is also influenced by the developments in understanding of the importance of the levitical, and especially Aaronic, priesthood current within first-century Judaism. This has been argued convincingly by Horbury (1983), who points to theocratic and hierocratic ideas in a variety of strands of Judaism in which the temple could be viewed as a microcosm of the cosmos and the Aaronic priests and the high priest had an exalted status because they were viewed as mediating God's rule over both Israel and the cosmos. This developed view of the priesthood had considerable political, social and economic implications. Horbury finds support for the proposal that the author of Hebrews was in touch with current notions about the priesthood and the sacrificial system from, for example, 7.5, which diverges from the Pentateuchal law of tithe in Num. 18.21 but is in line with first-century practice by assigning tithes to the priest in particular rather than the sons of Levi in general. Similarly, 9.13 links 'the blood of goats and bulls' from the Day of Atonement with 'the ashes of a heifer', which in the Pentateuch had no connection with that day. However, the two were associated in discussion and debate over Day of Atonement rites in the first century. Horbury's discussion also shows how the presuppositions of Hebrews 7–8 about the interdependence of the law and the priesthood, the subordination of law to priesthood and the decisive importance of the high priest reflect contemporary views and debates based on Pentateuchal material. The same holds for Hebrews' treatment of the ethical attributes of Christ as high priest in 2.17–3.1 and 4.14–5.10. Mercy, compassion, sympathy and solidarity with humanity are all prominent in discussions of the Aaronic priesthood and of the high priest in Jewish theocratic views. Hebrews, then, develops its views on the high priesthood of Christ not only through the exposition of the Scriptures but also in contact with developments in their interpretation in first-century Jewish thought and practice.

Qumran

Since the publication of the Dead Sea Scrolls various attempts have been made to link these writings with Hebrews. Some speculated that the readers were in fact former Essenes. More plausible were the suggestions of conceptual links. It was pointed out, for example, that angels have a role in the community's worship both in the Qumran writings (cf. 1QS 11.8) and in Hebrews (cf. 12.22). But this belief was more widespread and Hebrews need by no means have been dependent on Qumran for it. The same holds for other features, including exegetical techniques in interpreting Scripture, put forward in the initial enthusiasm for finding parallels between Qumran and Hebrews; they turn out to be not so much distinctive to Qumran as common to first-century Judaism. It is true that Qumran and Hebrews both contain a critique of the Jewish cult. But in terms of influence or dependence this is a relatively superficial observation. Qumran attacks the corruption of the Jerusalem priesthood in its own day, while Hebrews, more radically, sets out the deficiency of the whole cultic system even when its Scriptural foundations are in view. It is sometimes suggested that the argument of Hebrews may be directed against the expectation in the Scrolls that there would be two messiahs – a priestly or Aaronic one and a royal one. But the argument of Hebrews moves on a different plane in its attempt to show how Christ's royal sonship and high priesthood can be established. Its argument is directed against those who would hold to the permanence of the old cultic arrangements, not against opposing views of messiahship.

The later publication, in 1965, of the fragment 11Q Melchizedek, however, added fuel to attempts to show an association with Hebrews by revealing that special attention appears to have been paid to Melchizedek at Qumran. But again the treatments are quite distinct. In the fragment, Melchizedek is portrayed as a superior angel, who has a special relation to the law of jubilee and is charged with the duty of serving as a heavenly guardian and deliverer of the people of God. Hebrews shows no sign of having interacted with such a view. Its depiction of Melchizedek is as a human being and is based solely on the two scriptural passages where his name occurs. There is also no indication that Hebrews might have been arguing for Christ's superiority over against the exalted angelic role assigned to Melchizedek. At the most, 11Q Melchizedek provides evidence for renewed interest in this figure in the first century.

Middle Platonism and Philo

With its excellent Greek style, its use of the LXX, and its knowledge and effective employment of the techniques of rhetoric developed in the Graeco-Roman world, Hebrews reflects the convergence of Jewish and Greek cultural traditions. As in the case of the writings of some other educated Jews, there is little doubt that it is to be affiliated generally with Hellenistic Judaism. It is a further question, however, how far it is to be associated with that aspect of Hellenistic Judaism known as Middle Platonism. Plato (427–347 BCE) had formulated his ideas particularly through the dialogues in which Socrates is his mouthpiece. At the turn of the common era those ideas were influential through the development of his thought known as Middle Platonism. One of its key elements was a dualistic cosmology, in which this material world was viewed as transient and unstable in comparison with the invisible permanent world of ideal reality. What happened in the material world could be seen as insubstantial shadows and copies of the real world of beauty and truth. To find fulfilment and achieve their true destiny people needed, therefore, to escape from the physical world and return to their souls' true home in that other upper world. Philo (c. 20 BCE–50 CE), a Hellenistic Jew from Alexandria, was heavily influenced by this brand of Middle Platonism in his endeavours to integrate philosophy and the Scriptures in order to communicate the Jewish religious tradition in a way that might appeal to educated Greeks.

Scholarship on Hebrews has been polarized about whether the thought of Philo should be considered an influence on Hebrews and if so, to what extent. Some commentators, such as Moffatt (*A Critical and Exegetical Commentary on the Epistle to the Hebrews*, ICC, Edinburgh: T. and T. Clark, 1924) and Spicq (*L'Épitre aux Hébreux*, 2 vols, Paris: Gabalda, 1952–53), made Philo an indispensable key to the interpretation of Hebrews, and Dey (1975) held that Hebrews was a polemic against the notion of perfection and how it was to be achieved through intermediaries in the middle platonic philosophy exemplified by Philo. Others denied any such influence. Williamson (1970) wrote a 580-page monograph, in which he interacted with Spicq's arguments and concluded: '. . . it is possible that the Writer of Hebrews had never been a Philonist, had never read Philo's works, had never come under the influence of Philo directly or indirectly. This is the conclusion to which the evidence set out above in this study seems to me to point' (p. 579).

There are, however, a limited number (not nearly as many as has often been suggested) of formulations and conceptions in Hebrews that appear to bear some resemblance to Philo's thought. The prime examples include the contrast between the earthly shadow and the true heavenly reality in 8.2, 5 and 10.1, the notion of the earthly sanctuary being a mere copy or antitype of the true one in 9.24, and the cosmological contrast between created things that can be removed and a permanent transcendent realm that remains in 12.27. A closer examination of such passages, however, reveals that the resemblances are by no means as clear as some have thought. The contrast between the earthly and the true heavenly sanctuary in 8.2, 5 is not between the phenomenal and the ideal but between the symbol and the reality to which the symbol points. The 'shadow' here is again not the world of phenomena as an imperfect reflection from the ideal world above. Coupled with the term *hupodeigma*, which means sketch or outline rather than copy, it most likely refers to the preliminary or anticipatory reflection of the reality that lies ahead (see Hurst 1990: 13–17). This is precisely its force in 10.1, which speaks of the law having a shadow of the good things to come and not their true form. The actual term translated 'true form' in NRSV is 'image' (*eikōn*), but significantly Philo employs this term with the opposite connotation, that of the earthly perceptible copy of an imperceptible reality (see Hurst 1990: 19–20). Whether the term used in 9.24 – *antitupos* – means 'mere copy' (NRSV) is uncertain. It is not found with the meaning of a copy of an original imperceptible reality until the writings of Plotinus in the third century CE. It is employed three times in Philo, but there it has the force of 'resistant'. Here in Hebrews it may simply mean the lesser of two counterparts, where the first is the symbol and the second the reality to which it points. The force of the contrast in 12.27 is one of the most debated points and will be treated more fully in considering the eschatology of Hebrews. While some (e.g. Thompson 1982: 48–49) see this verse as sharing the Middle Platonism in which the invisible is more real than the visible and as reflecting an eschatology that has no place for a new heaven and earth, others (e.g. Lane 1991: 481–83) interpret it as essentially in line with traditional Jewish eschatology.

For the most part, then, similar terms in Hebrews and Philo have different connotations because they are part of quite different conceptual frameworks. In their views on such matters as cosmology, history, eschatology and revelation Philo and the writer to the Hebrews differ markedly. As will be pointed out in the later treatment of Hebrews' eschatology, for example, its writer can incorporate some formulations found in Middle

Platonism for his own purposes of stressing the ultimate and permanent qualities of salvation and its present focus in the heavenly world without abandoning mainstream Jewish expectations about the future. In addition, Philo's type of allegorizing treatment of Scripture is far removed from Hebrews' interpretation of Scriptural texts, even where Hebrews is at its most allegorical in 7.1–3. It is likely that best justice is done to the evidence in concluding that, in those instances where the writer of Hebrews employs terminology which appears to resemble Philo's, this is taken over from the linguistic and conceptual world of Middle Platonism, which the two reflect independently and very differently, and that there are no grounds for claiming direct influence of Philo on Hebrews.

Gnosticism

Due particularly to the 1939 study by Käsemann (ET 1984), which posited major Gnostic influences on Hebrews and suggested that these amounted to its promotion of a Gnostic view of Christianity, an interpretation of Hebrews in terms of Gnostic categories was prominent primarily within German scholarship. More recently, H. Koester (*Introduction to the New Testament*, Vol. 2, New York: de Gruyter, 2nd edn, 2000, pp. 275–80), has perpetuated this perspective by offering a variation, in which Hebrews itself shows some Gnostic influence but is in fact opposing Gnostic views among its readers. Such proposals are, however, now generally abandoned on three main grounds. (i) The earliest extant sources for Gnosticism are the Nag Hammadi texts, to be dated between the second and the fourth centuries CE. This means that earlier 'gnostic' trends need to be distinguished from any developed system of Gnosticism, such as that known from Nag Hammadi, and makes proposals relating such trends to first-century New Testament documents hazardous because of the lack of any clear evidence. (ii) There is an absence in Hebrews of any of the main distinguishing features of later Gnosticism, such as the creation of the world by a demi-urge, human beings possessing intrinsically a spark of the divine nature, this world as the prison of the soul, and salvation being achieved through knowledge of the self and the world. (iii) Where there are overlaps between Hebrews and Gnostic ideas, such as salvation being viewed as a journey or wandering through this world and its goal as a resting-place or homeland, Hebrews' treatment of them can be adequately explained on the basis of its exposition of the Jewish Scriptures and their development in apocalyptic writings, and in any case it elaborates on such themes within a very different historical and eschatological framework. Any similarities between Hebrews and ideas in later Gnostic texts are, therefore, far more likely to be the result of their independent development of a common Hellenistic Jewish heritage.

Honour/shame culture

An awareness of the cultural and social values reflected in Hebrews is another aspect of the knowledge of this text's first-century background that is important for interpretation. B. Malina (*The New Testament World*, Atlanta: John Knox, 1981) has underlined the significance of the honour/shame value system in the patron-client society of the Mediterranean world in the first century CE for understanding the New Testament in general and D. deSilva (1995) has followed up this approach with respect to Hebrews in particular.

Honour and shame were central to the life of the society in which the recipients of Hebrews found themselves. To honour a person was to judge that his or her attitudes or behaviour conformed to what society expected and to make public acknowledgment of this. Honour involved both one's own sense of worth and its public recognition, and was therefore clearly bound up with identity, and in first-century Mediterranean societies identity was a matter of both social identity and social recognition. On the individual level identity was closely associated with one's name, which represented one's public persona, one's reputation. But honour was important for both individuals and groups, and was what was vied for and gained at the expense of other individuals and groups. To have shame in such a society was evaluated positively because it meant having sensitivity to one's reputation and to questions of honour in human interaction. The negative aspects of the system were to be shameless, that is, to be lacking in respect for such social issues, and to be shamed, that is, to be denied honourable status by public opinion. One could be shamed by being rejected by one's own group or society, but also by one's own group being despised or dishonoured by some other group or by society as a whole. Social groups possessed a collective or corporate honour in which individuals shared, so that if a person's family or patron or god was affronted, that person's honour would be seen to be at stake and the attempt would need to be made to restore it. It should be clear then that honour and shame were not simply social symbols but represented social realities that were experienced at every level of social interaction.

As will be seen more fully later, one of the main issues facing the readers of Hebrews was the cost of their Christian confession – their loss of status and material goods, their marginalization by and threat of persecution from the wider society. If being shamed involved social humiliation, then the addressees had already experienced such shaming. Their earlier suffering entailed 'being publicly exposed to abuse and persecution, and sometimes being partners with those so treated' (10.33). Now they needed similar endurance to that which they had previously exhibited, and one of the ways in which the author encourages this is to instil in them a sense of the honour of being Christian believers and to encourage them to view the matter of shaming by others in a different light. Language associated with honour and shame is found throughout Hebrews and one of the major connotations of the term 'glory', employed in English translations, is honour or reputation. From the start the honour of the one to whom believers confess allegiance is stressed. He is the radiance of the divine glory and his honour is underlined by his exalted status – at the right hand of the majesty on high – and by comparison with the angels – he has a more excellent name (1.3, 4). This name is that of Son. Lineage played an important role in this system of values, so that people could be ascribed honour because of the family of origin into which they were born. It was in knowing whose child they were that others knew who they were and what honour to grant them. Jesus' supreme honour is seen in his being God's Son. But, in addition, a person of power could ascribe honour to another and compel public acknowledgment of such honour. This aspect also colours Hebrews' portrayal of Jesus. It is one who was a shamed and ignominiously executed person who is being ascribed honour by God. Crucifixion was, of course, the most shameful way to meet one's end and 12.2 explicitly speaks of shame in connection with the cross. Yet throughout the letter God is shown as promoting the honour of Jesus, whether in terms of the comparison with Moses (3.3) or in terms of his calling to be high priest (5.4, 5). In fact, Christ as high priest can be depicted as embodying God's word of honour. To eliminate ambiguity about whether a person's honour was at stake in a given interchange, resort was made to swearing or oath-taking as a means of giving one's word of honour. Here Christ's priesthood according to the order of Melchizedek constitutes the oath that God has sworn (6.16–18; 7.20–22, 28). What is more, in a reversal of values, Christ is 'now crowned with glory and honour' not simply despite suffering a humiliating death but because of it (2.9).

This pattern is to shape the readers' attitudes. If they want approval – in the eyes of the ultimate arbiter of honour – then it is faith that receives such approval (11.2, 4, 5, 39). And their exercise of faith will have as one of its models Moses, who chose 'to share ill-treatment with the people of God . . . and considered abuse suffered for the Christ to be greater wealth than the treasures of Egypt' (11.25, 26). Their supreme model will be Jesus himself, 'who for the sake of the joy set before him endured the cross, disregarding its shame, and has taken his seat at the right hand of the throne of God' (12.2). They will be encouraged in their endurance by the knowledge that they already share in Christ's ascribed family honour by having been made part of the same family with the same Father (2.11). Indeed, their pioneer 'is not ashamed to call them brothers and sisters' (2.11, 12) and will lead them to glory (2.10). A leader or teacher was honoured if his followers accepted his words, but was dishonoured if they rejected them and abandoned him. It is not surprising, then, that the warnings against falling away or rejecting the message in Hebrews are formulated in terms of the shame to which this would expose Christ. This course of action would entail 'crucifying again the Son of God and holding him up to contempt' (6.6). Instead of shaming him, the readers are meant to reflect on Jesus as the repository of God's honour and to become more fully aware that, as his family and followers, they share in his reputation. Instead of fearing society's opinion and seeking its approval, they have a different perspective on their role in the world. Honour for them will lie in having God's approval and in following Jesus, as they 'go to him outside the camp and bear the abuse he endured' (13.13).

Patron/client relationships

Exchanges of honour took place within a system of patron/client relationships in society. Patrons were the social superiors who controlled access to basic goods such as land, jobs, finances, citizenship and power. They showed favour to clients as social inferiors by making their patronage available to them as needed. In return clients were obliged to enhance the honour and prestige of the patron in private and in public. They did so by such means as offering greetings in public, supplying support and information, refusing to testify against a patron, and consistently bearing witness to their patron's benefactions. Some institutional and legal arrangements were shaped by the patron–client relationship, but for the most part it was a social contract into which one entered voluntarily. It was then, however, considered mutually binding and, ideally, lifelong. The acceptance of a patron's gift or favour was also the acceptance, on the part of a client, of the obligation of gratitude. The reciprocal favour/ obligation relationship was typical of that between the head of a family and his dependents – wives, children, slaves. In fact, it produced an overarching network of kinship in which the patron saw clients as dependents and clients related to patrons as more powerful family heads. The other important figure in this system was the broker who mediated between patrons situated above and clients located below in this hierarchical relationship. Brokers manipulated their own network of contacts to put clients in touch with significant patrons, and again this would be done in exchange for services, goodwill, information or honour. Social brokerage could become a competitive affair and involve playing off patrons against each other.

Not surprisingly, the various elements of this pervasive system coloured the way in which divine–human relationships were conceived. In Judaism and in early Christianity God would be thought of as the ultimate patron, the controller of all goods who had the power to confer favour or grace.

God had taken the initiative to establish a patron–client relationship with particular peoples, Israel and the Church, and in doing so had made use of brokers such as Moses, the prophets or Jesus. The more traditional categories – Lord, covenant, mediator – were readily accommodated to or understood in terms of such social roles and arrangements. In Hebrews God is clearly the ultimate patron and benefactor. Jesus functions as the broker (cf. 8.6; 9.15; 12.24), who provides access to this patron (cf. 4.14–16; 10.19–22), his grace (4.16) and the good things that have come (9.11). As the Son, Jesus is so much at one with the patron that he can also be seen as conferring divine benefactions as he comes to the aid of human clients (cf. 2.16). As clients, believers owe gratitude and praise (cf. 12.28; 13.15). But if client praise honours the patron, then client disloyalty and the refusal of gifts and favours dishonours the patron, and so here in Hebrews turning one's back on good gifts (cf. 6.4–6), for example, calls into question the divine honour and reputation. Clearly loyalty to or trust in the patron is very important. This is reflected in the letter's treatment of faith, where entailed in such loyalty is the willingness to believe that the promises of future rewards and benefactions offered by the patron can be trusted and are worth the costs involved while waiting for them (cf. 6.12–18; 10.35, 36; 11.6, 26).

Further reading

On authorship and date, see Trotter 1997: 27–57; Salevao 2002: 95–108.

On Rome as the probable location of the recipients, see R. E. Brown and J. P. Meier, *Antioch and Rome* (Ramsey, NJ: Paulist, 1983), pp. 140–57; Salevao 2002: 118–21.

On a developed view of priesthood, see W. Horbury, 'The Aaronic Priesthood in the Epistle to the Hebrews', *JSNT* 19 (1983), pp. 43–71.

On the general conceptual background of Hebrews, see the monograph of Hurst 1990.

On Philo and Middle Platonism in particular, see the monograph of Thompson 1982 and also K. L. Schenk, 'Philo and the Epistle to the Hebrews: Ronald Williamson's Study after Thirty Years', *Studia Philonica Annual* 14 (2002), pp. 112–35.

On the cultural and social values reflected in Hebrews, see the monograph by deSilva 1995.

5

Occasion and Purposes

It was noted in the earlier discussions of the genre and rhetoric of Hebrews and of the structure of its argument that the sections of exposition in this epistle always lead into and serve the hortatory sections that follow. The exposition sections are all variations on the theme of the comparison between the previous stage of God's revelation to Israel and the final and superior stage of that revelation in Christ. The purposes of such theological exposition and of Hebrews as a whole are most clearly revealed, therefore, in its paraenetic passages, where it addresses its audience most directly. There are warnings of the dangers of drifting away from the message the addressees have heard (2.1–4) and of falling through unbelief and disobedience (3.7–4.13). These are followed by exhortations to hold fast to their confession (4.14–16) and to move beyond the basics of Christian teaching to maturity and not to become sluggish or to fall away (5.11–6.12). The lengthy central exposition concludes with an exhortation to appropriate the access to God provided by Christ and to hold fast the confession without wavering, together with a warning about the consequences of deliberately persisting in sin or shrinking back (10.19–39). The last part of the letter contains an extensive encouragement to faith and endurance (11.1–12.17), a final warning not to refuse God's message in Christ alongside an exhortation to be thankful (12.25–29), and further concluding exhortations to love and good works (13.1–19).

In the light of such hortatory material, one can return to the earlier brief treatment of rhetorical exigency or *stasis* and sum up the problem that the preacher sees as needing to be overcome as one involving the temptation to become discouraged and to drift away from or even reject the Christian confession, a problem that he believes has its ultimate roots in unbelief and disobedience. Correspondingly, the overall purpose of his message can be seen as urging its hearers to hold fast to their confession of faith in Jesus who, as Son of God and high priest, is God's final and decisive word in comparison with earlier revelation. That message tells them that holding fast to the confession of faith will entail costly endurance on the way to participating in the completed salvation of the world to come but that falling away or apostasizing will have dire consequences in terms of God's judgement.

Put in these terms, such an exhortation might be addressed to any group of Christians who were becoming discouraged or losing conviction about their Christian confession, and the epistle has certainly transcended its original setting and been read effectively as speaking to such general needs. Two more recent studies have attempted to be more specific about the document's situation and purpose by employing social-scientific methods. Using Mary Douglas' group/grid analysis of societies, Johnson (2001) concludes that the ideal society implied by Hebrews is weak in terms of both group and grid. He infers from this that the purpose of its critique of the Levitical system is to enable the addressees to be willing to engage with outsiders and to incorporate converts into the community. It is by no means obvious, however, given the lack of specific data with which to work in the case of Hebrews, that this method is entirely appropriate for discovering anything more concrete about the specific situation of the letter's actual recipients, and its conclusion about the writer's main purpose is more dependent on the theory applied than on the textual data, running counter to the clear indications about the writer's persuasive aims that lie on the surface of the argument and have been outlined above.

In a more wide-ranging discussion that attempts 'to put the body and soul of Hebrews together again' (414), Salevao (2002) provides a comprehensive treatment of the symbolic universe of Hebrews. His suggestion about the socio-historical situation of the readers (121–64) stays closer to the textual data and overlaps with that offered below. He attempts to fill out some of the details with the help of conflict theory, but dependence on the latter and on the application of the typology of a sect may have contributed unduly to his dubious characterization of the author's treatment of Jewish tradition as 'very hostile' rather than simply negative (218). Salevao's overall conclusion about the purpose or function of the letter's theology in terms of seeking to legitimate, through elaborate self-definition, the sectarian separation of the Hebrews community from local Jewish synagogues is eminently plausible. Both the doctrine of the impossibility of a second repentance and the major superiority/ inferiority comparisons are explained as maintaining the symbolic universe erected to legitimate the community (250). Salevao is very well aware of the danger of reducing theological to sociological explanations. It can, however, be questioned whether it is a sufficient explanation to claim that the author's stress on the superiority of the new covenantal order 'was dictated by the nature of the socio-historical situation of the readers' (356). The strong core conviction about the superiority of the Christian symbolic universe to the inherited Jewish one must have existed prior to its elaboration here in order for the writer and his readers to have made their Christian confession in the first place.

While acknowledging the value of judicious use of social-scientific models for organizing textual data, the following discussion will attempt to follow up the clues offered by the document itself about the more specific dimensions of the situation of the original Christian readers and the purpose of its urgent exhortation, without direct dependence on particular models but also without separating the soul and body of Hebrews. Again, the clues about the occasion are clearest in the paraenetical sections of the letter, but once these have been considered, it is also necessary to assess whether the long sections of exposition may shed additional light on the readers' setting. Picking up on such clues in order to depict the situation facing the addressees inevitably involves a certain amount of what has come to be called 'mirror-reading' of the text, that is, the drawing of inferences about that situation from the language and formulations used by the writer both in his exhortations and in his assertions about Christ and his work. The circularity entailed need not be considered entirely vicious, provided that such inferences are employed to fill out the picture already obtained from more direct evidence and that the procedure is carried out cautiously (cf. also Salevao 2002: 166–69).

Occasion

Proceeding in this way, and aware that the perspective on their situation is that of the writer, it is possible to see the issues the recipients faced as falling into three broad categories which overlap and affect each other.

Suffering, persecution, social marginalization and fear of death

The addressees belong to a community that had already experienced a wave of persecution. They had 'endured a hard struggle with sufferings, sometimes being publicly exposed to abuse and persecution, and sometimes being partners with those so treated'. At this time some had experienced imprisonment and others the plundering of their possessions (10.32–34). Having weathered that storm they were now, however, facing further testing. Some of them were at present in prison and being tortured (13.3). In attempting to brace the readers for continuing endurance, the writer asserts, 'In your struggle against sin you have not yet resisted to the point of shedding your blood' (12.4). In context, this is a reminder that in their testing they have not been pushed to the limits endured by their pioneer, Jesus (cf. 12.2), and so have no grounds for shrinking back in the face of lesser suffering. It may, however, also indicate that the writer believed fiercer persecution to be a possibility for them. It is significant that his pre-ceding treatment of heroes and heroines of faith is concerned not simply to highlight their faith but also, in several instances, their faith in relation-ship to death. In 11.4 Abel's faith brought about his death, but death did not have the last word – he had received approval as righteous and, though he died, through his death he still speaks. In 11.13 the faith of the patri-archs is summed up in terms of their all having 'died in faith without having received the promises'. Their experiencing of death before any fulfilment of the promises made to them did not mean any calling into question of the validity of those promises. Abraham's faith in offering up Isaac is also formulated in terms of his conviction that death would not have the final say: 'he considered the fact that God is able even to raise someone from the dead – and figuratively speaking, he did receive him back' (11.19). In par-ticular, 11.34–39 tell of faith in the face of severe persecution and violent death – by fire, by the sword, by stoning. Again, as 11.35b indicates, such faith entailed belief in the resurrection – 'others were tortured, refusing to accept release [on the condition of renouncing their faith], in order to obtain a better resurrection [not just a temporary return to mortal life – cf. v. 35a]'.

It may well be, then, that these emphases have been made because the writer believes that a renewed threat of persecution is imminent and is aware that the prospect of death for some is a realistic one that has inevitably provoked an accompanying fear. Other references add support to this reconstruction of the situation. Early on there is talk of those 'held in slavery by the fear of death' (2.15), and the depiction of Jesus' testing mentions his loud cries and tears in the face of impending death (5.7). Then the last citation of Scripture in the sermon is from Ps. 118.6, a psalm which celebrates God's help in the face of hostility and death (cf. Ps. 118.10–18) and which here in its new context speaks to the fear of death – 'The Lord is my helper; I will not be afraid. What can anyone do to me?' (13.6).

To face death for confessing their faith is a possible ultimate test for the readers, but in the present they are also being confronted with persecution in its more everyday guise as persistent mistreatment, social humiliation and marginalization. At this point the discussion in the previous chapter of the frequency of terminology associated with honour/glory, on the one hand, and shame/abuse, on the other, should be recalled. The addressees had had a major experience of being exposed to public abuse and affliction (10.33). They had been publicly shamed for their confession of faith. It is in the context of a reminder of this experi-ence that the writer calls on the readers not to abandon their boldness or confidence and to continue to endure. The social stigma resulting from loss of property and status, from verbal denunciations and contempt, and from associating with prisoners, was wearing and dispiriting and the pressure to be ashamed of their association with a despised community was strong. Again, as noted earlier, the writer's formulations reflect his awareness of this aspect of his readers' testing. Jesus, as their exemplar, was willing to disregard shame and to bear hostility and abuse (12.2, 3; 13.13). Moses was willing 'to share ill-treatment with the people of God' and 'considered abuse suffered for the Christ to be greater wealth than the treasures of Egypt' (11.25, 26). The readers are urged not to neglect meeting with their fellow believers or showing solidarity with imprisoned and tortured believers (10.25; 13.3). If they are tempted to be ashamed of such an association, they are reminded both that God is not ashamed to be called the God of those who exercise faith (11.16) and that Jesus is not ashamed to call believers his brothers and sisters (2.11). From the perspective of the writer, the real question in regard to social humiliation, as in regard to physical persecution and possible martyrdom, is whose approval, judgement and reward ultimately count – those of God or those of humans.

Discouragement, eschatological uncertainty and insecurity

The readers' need for endurance would not only have been due to external opposition and pressure, although it may well have been brought on and exacerbated by these. The letter suggests other symptoms of discouragement. Among these are a diminished commitment and an accompanying stunted growth in understanding. The readers have to be exhorted to hold their confidence and confession firm and not to waver (cf. 3.6, 14; 10.23). They are in danger of shrinking back (10.38, 39). Not only has their comprehension become dull so that they remain stuck on the basics of Christian teaching (5.11; 6.1) but they are also becoming sluggish (6.12). The imagery of 'drooping hands' and 'weak knees' is employed for the flabbiness of their resolve, which needs to be stiffened (12.12). The writer is aware that such discouragement can lead to disbelief and disobedience (3.12; 4.11) and from there to a wilful persistence in sin and to falling away altogether (6.6; 10.26).

Such discouragement may well have been fuelled by a sense of eschatological uncertainty among the addressees. Hebrews' formulations reflect the eschatological ideas the readers would have shared with other early Christians. They had put their faith in Jesus as the Messiah who had inaugurated the end-times (cf. 'in these last days' – 1.2; 'at the end of the age' – 9.26). They confessed him as the one who had brought in the salvation of the world to come or the age to come (cf. 2.5; 6.5). Such a confession must have looked fragile in the midst of their testing. How could they be experiencing the salvation of the coming age when the opposition was so clearly in control, and further suffering and even death were real possibilities? What sort of messianic age was this when their Messiah had gone to heaven and left them to face shaming and humiliation, and any claims of his imminent return had failed to materialize? Confusion and doubt were contributing to their general malaise. Three times the writer stresses the need for eagerly awaiting the parousia of Christ or the day of the Lord (9.26; 10.25, 37, 38), the concept of hope is emphasized (cf. 3.6; 6.11, 18, 19; 7.19; 10.23; 11.1), and much of the rest of the argument, including the elaboration on Christ's high priestly ministry, as we shall see, is framed in terms of coping with the interim period – the time between the inauguration and the consummation of the coming age.

Since many of the benefits of faith in Jesus still lay in the future, accompanying the uncertainty there would also have been a sense of insecurity and impermanence. Holding firm to the confession about Christ appeared to be a risky business in comparison with the securities of the allegiances that had been left behind. It is significant that, when Abraham's faith is depicted, he is portrayed as not knowing where he was going, as an alien, as seeking a more permanent country (cf. 11.8–10, 13–16) and that the writer has earlier been at pains to contrast the impermanence of the arrangements under the law with the permanent and lasting consequences of Christ's priesthood (cf. 7.23, 24).

Temptation to turn back from the Christian confession (to Judaism)

The temptation on the part of some of the addressees to drift away or turn back from their Christian confession is clear (cf. e.g. 2.1; 3.12; 6.4–6; 10.35, 39). What is not spelled out is to what they are drifting or turning back. The traditional view – that they were contemplating a return to the beliefs and practices of Judaism – has come in for criticism from some more recent scholarship, primarily because it is not mentioned explicitly in the letter and has to be inferred. The problem, of course, as with much of the discussion of Hebrews' setting, is that writer and readers could assume mutual knowledge of the major features of the latter's situation, which did not, therefore, need to be mentioned directly. The questions, then, become whether a hypothesis that draws inferences about that situation does justice to what is said indirectly, and which hypothesis illumines and makes best sense of the whole of the letter's message. As will be suggested below, there are strong reasons for maintaining the traditional view. Nevertheless, parentheses have been placed around 'to Judaism' in the sub-heading above as a reminder that this view does remain an inference, even if the most plausible one.

As regards the overall argument of the letter, Hebrews is pervaded by the comparison and contrast between two dispensations of revelation, the old covenant and the new covenant, stressing the superiority of the latter. As has already been acknowledged, in theory this could just be theologizing which does not necessarily have a direct relevance to the audience's situation. But it makes much more sense in this pastoral word of exhortation that such a massive interest in the relationship of the two dispensations does in fact have a bearing on the concrete situation of those whom the writer is attempting to help by dissuading them from a disastrous drift away from their new confession.

The hypothesis of a temptation to return to their previous allegiance to Judaism does, in fact, make very good sense in the light of the discussion of both of the previous aspects of the addressees' situation. There can be little doubt that the persecution and social pressures experienced by the readers would have been eased by such a move. Jewish Christians were in a highly ambiguous relation to the Roman state. While Judaism was a protected religion, the Christian movement was frequently viewed by Roman officials as another religion that was potentially subversive of the household and the state and that refused to participate in state cults that honoured the Roman gods. The Roman historian, Tacitus, could call it a 'pernicious superstition' (*Annals* 15). Jewish Christians faced the choice of identifying themselves primarily as Jews or primarily as Christians, and the decision would have made a significant difference in terms of social status and security. Payment of the Jewish tax, the *fiscus Judaicus*, also forced the issue and frequently led to denunciation of both Jews and Christians. Roman officials had to decide who was Jewish and therefore liable to the tax. Suetonius (*Domitian* 12.2) reports that the tax was 'levied with the utmost rigour and those were prosecuted who without publicly acknowledging that faith yet lived as Jews as well as those who concealed their origin and did not pay the tribute levied upon their people'. If Jewish Christians were unable to evade the tax, this may have contributed further to the feeling that they might as well return to Judaism as their primary allegiance anyway.

Eschatological confusion and uncertainty is also most adequately explained by positing Jewish Christians as the addressees. It is such believers who would have had inculcated from their heritage the clearest notions of what was expected with the arrival of the Messiah and would have sensed most sharply the disappointment when not only did these fail to materialize but there was also no sign of any fulfilment of the Christian adjustment, whereby the Messiah would come a second time. Given their suffering of the practical difficulties as well as their doubts about the new Christian set of eschatological convictions, it would have been easier to revert to their original expectations and find some other way of fitting any remaining attraction to Jesus into their belief system.

The question is often raised why Hebrews contains such a lengthy comparison between the Son and the angels in 1.4–14. Clearly the primary function of this material is to serve the contrast between the two dispensations of revelation, as 2.2, 3 make explicit. The angels were held to be mediators of the revelation of the law (cf. also Gal. 3.19; Acts 7.53; Josephus, *Ant.* 15.136), and if disobedience in the face of that revelation had its penalties, how much more is this the case with the new and final revelation given in a Son? But if one looks for a secondary reason why so much space is given to the contrast with angels in the very first chapter, then the most satisfactory may well be that some of the readers were in danger, in their drift away from the full-blown confession as Christ as Son, of compromising by conceiving of him as on the level of an angelic intermediary. This is in fact one of the ways in which Jesus came to be viewed in some segments of Jewish Christianity. The second-century Ebionites treated Jesus as either a prophet or an angel. Epiphanius (*Panarion* 30.16.3–4; cf. also *Ep. Apost.* 14) later reported the Ebionites' claim that Christ was 'not begotten by God the Father, but created as one of the archangels'. Hebrews, then, would be dismissing any such suggestion by underlining that Christ as the Son has a status and title far superior to those of any angel – 'For to which of the angels did God ever say, "You are my Son; today I have begotten you"?' (1.5).

Two complementary variations on the traditional perspective on the readers' situation have more recently been offered in its support. Lindars (1991) focuses on the problem of the readers' consciousness of sin or their guilty conscience. As the argument of the letter progresses to its climax, there are several references to this issue (cf. 9.9, 10, 14; 10.2, 22; cf. also 13.18). To explain this emphasis, Lindars posits that diaspora Jewish Christians were finding the early Christian proclamation of forgiveness of sins through Christ liturgically and emotionally unsatisfying. They had become oppressed by a continuing consciousness of sin, which the Christian gospel did not seem clearly to allow for or cope with, whereas they had been accustomed from their Jewish heritage for this matter to be continually attended to, particularly through the ceremonies associated with the Day of Atonement.

One might also want to underline that it would be particularly difficult for Jewish Christians to break with habits of thought and ways of self-identification in regard to sin and a holy God that had been long ingrained. Lindars offers an interpretation of 13.9, 10 in support of this proposal, in which the strange teachings, entailing regulations about food and associated with 'those who officiate in the tent', that is, the Levitical priests, are seen as referring to regulations about meals linked with atonement rites (cf. also 9.10). For diaspora Jews such meals were held in the synagogue at festival times and produced a sense of solidarity with the temple cult and its sacrificial system. This specific aspect of Lindars' case might seem to depend on a date for the epistle when the central atonement rituals in the Jerusalem temple were still being celebrated. This need not necessarily be so, however, since even after the fall of Jerusalem activities such as meals, fasting and special prayers became a substitute for actual sacrifices and gave a tangible sense that atonement for sins was being addressed. Whatever one makes of the details of Lindars' reconstruction (and there is no clear evidence for the nature of diaspora celebrations of the Day of Atonement during this period), his proposal does have the merit of highlighting the writer's emphatic argument about the continuing efficacy of the work of Christ in relation to sin and the conscience, and of suggesting a possible context for this.

Gordon (2000) also sees a more general sense of what he calls 'cultic deprivation' as part of the Jewish Christian addressees' problem. In this regard he finds it significant that the writer stresses several times what Christian believers 'have'. Such references include their having a great high priest who is able to sympathize (4.14, 15; 8.1; 10.21), having right of access to the sanctuary of a holy God through Christ's offering of himself (10.19), and having an altar of their own, the sacrifice of Christ, to which those who operate in the merely tangible realm of the earthly tabernacle have no access (13.10). These assertions serve to counter perceptions of their cultic impoverishment on the part of some who are attracted by the more tangible aspects of their Jewish heritage. To this one might add that the crucial distinction in the law between what was clean and what was unclean had palpable, material and physical consequences, and that Hebrews' stress on the reality of the spiritual and invisible in contrast to the material and earthly in parts of the argument, not least the climactic 12.18–29 (cf. 'you have not come to something that can be touched'), also makes sense of the temptation to return to the rituals of the ancestral religion.

Purposes

If what has been suggested above bears some approximation to the issues that provided the occasion for Hebrews, then, when an attempt is made to elaborate on the earlier more general statement about the preacher's overall purpose, one would expect the more specific features to be related to such issues. Indeed, aspects of his proposed solutions have already been mentioned in the depiction of the problems. And just as the various aspects of the occasion overlap, so do the sermon's responses. The issues are not dealt with separately but are intertwined in various ways throughout the argument and exhortation. Nevertheless, particular passages can be seen to address one of the aspects in a more focused fashion. The following presentation of the purposes will, therefore, feature one section of the sermon in particular, while not neglecting mention of other places in this 'word of exhortation' that are relevant to an appreciation of the purpose being treated. The purposes to be highlighted, then, are part of the writer's pastoral response to the perceived situation and reflect the conviction that a more adequate understanding of the person and work of Christ and of their implications is what is required if the crisis the addressees face is to be overcome. In pursuing his pastoral and Christological purposes, the writer begins as he means to continue. The opening *exordium* draws on confessional material to make a number of statements about Christ's significance in the cosmos, in relation to God and in salvation, and these are prefaced by the assertion that this Christ of the confession is the Son who is God's word. In this way, although sympathizing with the problems the addressees face, he directs them away from their external circumstances and internal doubts and fears and attempts to place these in perspective by focusing on Christ. He asks his readers to pay attention to God's word in the Son (2.1; cf. 1.2) and will go on to talk of seeing Jesus (2.9), looking to Jesus (12.2) and considering Jesus (12.3). Both aural and visual metaphors, hearing and seeing, are employed for the response the writer is seeking. By directing them to listen to God's word in Jesus, his sermon is also designed to enable the readers to see Jesus more clearly and therefore to have a renewed and sustaining vision of what a life of confessing him entails.

Jesus as the solution to suffering, persecution, social marginalization and fear of death

In 2.5–18 the writer employs LXX Psalm 8, read in the light of the new situation in Christ, as a word of exhortation that addresses the tension the readers are experiencing between the inauguration of the world to come and their continuing suffering, dishonour and persecution. His point is that all things are meant to be subject to humanity, as the psalm asserts, but if humanity is understood in the light of *the* man, Jesus, light is shed on how to live with the tension of this not yet being the case. 'We do not yet see everything in subjection' (2.8), as would be expected in the world to come (cf. 2.5). 'But we do see Jesus . . .' (2.9), who represents the 'already' of the coming world's salvation. Does the psalm say of humans that God has 'crowned them with glory and honour' (cf. 2.7)? God has kept this promise about human destiny through Jesus. The one who entered the human sphere and is now exalted to God's right hand is the representative human who *has* been crowned with glory and honour. For those who might be inclined to object that that may be the case for Jesus but they have been left to experience suffering and dishonour, the writer adds a further observation. Jesus received his exalted status not in spite of but 'because of the suffering of death' and thereby tasted death for everyone, removing its sting (2.9). There will be glory and honour for believers too – God is bringing many sons and daughters to glory (2.10) – but it should not now be surprising if they have to travel the same route to glory as their pioneer, the hero or champion who has blazed the trail (cf. also 12.2) and who was perfected through suffering. Though they may be tempted to be ashamed of their confession of him and their association with other believers, he is not ashamed to call them his brothers and sisters (2.11b). The purpose of his incarnation was for him to become the sort of champion who could take on and overcome the champion of sin and death, the devil, and thereby liberate people who were in slavery to the fear of death (2.14, 15). The readers will still have to go through death themselves, but if the fear of death is paralyzing them and they are losing their grip on their Christian confession, they need to focus on the one who has taken the fear out of death and made it instead their path to honour and glory. The end of this passage, in 2.17, 18, brings Jesus' high priesthood into the picture. His exaltation to God's right hand does not mean that he is now removed and remote from what the readers are experiencing. Rather, his suffering not only prepared him for glory but also prepared him to be the sort of high priest he is. His identification with his brothers and sisters in having suffered makes him a merciful and faithful high priest who is well able to help those who are tested, because he knows what such testing is like.

A large part of the purpose of Hebrews' development of its high priestly Christology is a response to this aspect of the occasion. In 4.14–5.10 Jesus' high priesthood is seen as bridging the gap between his exaltation to heaven and the human experience of suffering. The high priest who has passed through the heavens is not someone who is unable to sympathize with human weaknesses but someone who in every respect has been tested and tempted as humans are and yet remained without sin (4.14, 15). In fact, 5.7–10 graphically depict as one of Jesus' qualifications for priesthood how he went through the gruelling experience of facing death and, with loud cries and tears, asked to be saved from it. He confronted an experience of apparent abandonment and knows therefore what the sort of testing that can result in disillusionment is all about. Yet he endured this in obedience and, having been made perfect through his suffering, has become the source of the readers' salvation and of help for them in time of need (cf. 4.16). It is this Jesus who is high priest and whose help will not necessarily take believers out of suffering, shaming or death but will bring them through it. Again, the pattern of his life is to become theirs, as they look 'to Jesus, the pioneer and perfecter of our faith, who for the sake of the joy that was set before him endured the cross, disregarding its shame, and has taken his seat at the right hand of the throne of God' (12.2).

Jesus as the solution to discouragement, eschatological uncertainty and insecurity

The second aspect of the addressees' problem has already been partially answered in 2.5–18 in the way it depicts Jesus, the representative human and the high priest, as spanning the tension between the 'already' and the 'not yet' of the salvation of the world to come. But the further depiction of Jesus' high priestly role in 6.13–7.28 also speaks to this matter. The writer wants his readers to replace discouragement with the hope or confident assurance that God will fulfil God's purposes for the world's salvation. In 6.13, therefore, he takes up the notion of God swearing an oath, as he lays the groundwork for pointing out that one of his key texts about the Melchizedek priesthood, Ps. 110.4, already introduced in 5.6, 10, also involves an oath. This first instance in Scripture of God's oath-taking has Abraham as recipient. God pledged Godself to the death to keep the promise to Abraham. This, says the writer, shows it is absolutely impossible for God to prove false to what God has promised (6.17, 18a). Such an assertion addresses the very issue faced by the readers – are there grounds for trusting the claim about the eschatological promises being fulfilled in Christ, since the world to come has not arrived as expected? The writer explicitly points out that this quality of assurance was not just for Abraham but also for the heirs of the promise, who include himself and his readers – 'so that through two unchangeable things [God's promise and God's oath] . . . we who have taken refuge might be strongly encouraged to seize the hope set before us' (6.18). This moves the discussion from the promise-oath to Abraham to the form in which believers now have the assurance of this promise-oath. They have it embodied in Jesus' exaltation to heaven and his presence there as high priest for ever according to the order of Melchizedek (6.19, 20). In this way Jesus also provides the answer to their sense of insecurity and impermanence. As this type of high priest, who remains for ever, he is 'a sure and steadfast anchor of the soul', their immoveable and unbreakable link to the permanent heavenly realm.

Towards the end of his elaboration on Melchizedek's superiority to the Levitical priesthood, the writer claims that, in contrast to that priesthood's concern with physical descent, Jesus' new Melchizedek priesthood, through his resurrection and exaltation, is based on the power of an indestructible life and therefore introduces a better hope (7.15–19). Now this section of the argument can return to the image with which it started, that of God swearing an oath. The better hope represented by Jesus' Melchizedek priesthood is based on an oath. In the words of Ps. 110.4, 'The Lord has sworn and will not change his mind, "You are a priest for ever"' (7.20, 21). The force for the readers is that God has given them a permanently living oath – Jesus as high priest – to guarantee the divine promises of a better covenant, and it is he who serves as their security and confidence. This imagery connects back to the opening of the letter where the Son was seen as God's final and decisive word (1.2). The point is now made even more forcefully. God has not only spoken in the Son, God has also gone on oath in this Son as high priest. To its discouraged addressees this passage is saying that God has given a word of honour, in which the divine reputation is at stake, and because that word consists of what has taken place in Jesus, God cannot ever go back on the promise of the salvation of the world to come. The exaltation of Jesus to heaven as high priest is God's absolute oath and therefore the foundation for assured hope.

Other passages will make a similar point about the need to replace discouragement, doubt and insecurity with confident resolve and endurance in the light of God's assurance in Jesus. If they endure, believers will 'receive what was promised' (10.36). In its original context, Hab. 2.1–4 had functioned as part of a reassurance of God's future victory over evil when the prophet had complained about the fate of the righteous at the hands of the wicked and their violence. Now the words of LXX Hab. 2.3, read through the lens of God's word in Jesus, function in a similar way for mistreated and persecuted believers – 'in a very little while, the one who is coming will come and will not delay' (10.37). In the meanwhile they are to be assured that Jesus and the salvation he has accomplished are permanent realities. Heaven and earth may perish but he remains and is the same yesterday, today and for ever (cf. 1.10–12; 13.8). The death he died was once for all and confers secure and lasting benefits (cf. 9.12; 10.34; 12.26–28). But endurance is encouraged not only by looking to Jesus' second coming and to the eternal qualities of his person and work in heaven but also by reflecting on his pattern of life in his first appearance. 'Consider him who endured such hostility against himself from sinners, so that you may not grow weary or lose heart' (12.3). Indeed, following Jesus' pattern by enduring the trials of shaming and persecution can be seen as already a sign of honour, because it marks believers out as members of God's family, legitimate children rather than bastards (12.7, 8). There is every reason, therefore, for them to lift their drooping hands and strengthen their weak knees in order to run the race with perseverance (12.12; cf. 12.1c).

Jesus as the solution to the temptation to turn back from the Christian confession (to Judaism)

The lack of any explicit treatment of that to which the readers would be returning if they abandoned their confession serves as a reminder that, for the most part, the writer's primary purpose is not to denigrate the object of their former allegiance but to stress the superiority and finality of the content of their present confession. His focus is on the decisive significance of the Christian confession about Christ, and therefore also on the severe sanctions that would follow from rejecting it, and not on their experience of a return to past religious attachments. Nevertheless, if it is correct to infer that the readers are Jewish Christians and that therefore an abandoning of their confession would entail a merging back into Judaism, then much of the argument about the superiority of the revelation in Christ can be seen to speak to this perceived problem.

The long passage that runs from 8.1 to 10.18 can be singled out as one that is particularly pertinent as part of the writer's response to the readers' temptation to turn back in this way. The comparison of the two covenants in 8.1–13 sums up and takes further the comparison between the two dispensations of revelation earlier in the argument. As high priest according to the order of Melchizedek, Jesus is said to have a more excellent ministry than that of the Levitical priests and to be the mediator of a better covenant enacted though better promises (8.6). The very fact that a new covenant was prophesied, in which the law would be written on the heart and sins would be remembered no more, is seen to show the deficiencies of the first one, and now that the new covenant has been inaugurated, it is claimed not that the first one is still valid yet less adequate but rather that it is obsolete and about to disappear (8.13). The implication is plain – why would anyone turn their back on the new and find attractive the old arrangement which was unable to deal adequately with the problem of sin and which is on its way out?

The comparison between the arrangements under the first and those under the new covenant continues (9.1, 15) and the focus is on the issues of the forgiveness of sins and the cleansing of the conscience which, as noted earlier, appear to be troubling the readers and causing them to consider their Jewish heritage with its Day of Atonement in some ways more satisfactory in this regard. The writer claims that the very existence of a tent, in which access to its inner sanctum was restricted to the high priest once a year on the Day of Atonement, indicates the need for disclosure of a more direct way of access to the divine presence (9.8). Interestingly, he reduces the scope of the forgiveness available under the old arrangement to 'the sins committed unintentionally by the people' (9.7; cf. Lev. 16.16 – 'all their sins'). Even on this view, he is concerned to point out that the gifts and sacrifices that are offered 'cannot perfect the conscience of the worshipper but deal only with food and drink and various baptisms, regulations for the body imposed until the time comes to set things right' (9.9, 10). In the light of these perceived limitations of the old arrangements, which even the Day of Atonement evidences, the writer can now present Christ as entering into the heavenly holy place itself through his own blood and obtaining a redemption that partakes of the qualities of the age to come by being 'eternal' (9.12).

For those who remain attracted to a tangible and visible cult, it is emphasized that Christ's entry into heaven takes him through a superior sphere, for it is not 'made with hands', a term which in the LXX and else-where in the New Testament has pejorative overtones, and is not 'of this creation', that is, it does not belong to the present visible world which, in any case, is dependent for its existence on the invisible realm (cf. 11.3) and is headed for destruction (cf. 12.27). At this point in the argument the con-centration of terms emphasizing the continuing and permanent efficacy of Christ's work is striking. For any having problems with a persistent con-sciousness of sin, not only is redemption through Christ said to be eternal, but his achievement, in contrast to the annual Day of Atonement arrange-ments, is once for all time, needing no repetition (*ephapax* – 9.12), is secured through the eternal Spirit, and is therefore able to 'purify our con-science from dead works to worship the living God' (9.14). As mediator of the new covenant, Christ enables the receipt of the promise of 'the eternal inheritance' (9.15), which only a deliberate rejection by turning back can put in jeopardy.

The same key points about how Christ's death deals with sin are repeated at the end of chapter 9. Christ has appeared, on behalf of sinful and defiled humans, in the very presence of God, not in a sanctuary made by human hands, which is only symbolic of the true one. And, unlike the Aaronic high priest, he does not do this annually or again and again, since this would mean his repeated suffering (9.24–26a). Rather there is an eschatological quality to his activity. It entails the decisive removal of sins because it occurs 'at the end of the ages' and is efficacious once for all time (9.26b). In a formulation that may recall the Day of Atonement, when to the eager expectation and relief of the worshippers the high priest returned from the sanctuary, signalling the divine approval of the sacri-fice, it is said that Christ, having made his offering, will appear a second time for the salvation of those who eagerly await him. Unlike his first appearance, his return will have nothing to do with atonement for sin, because that issue has been fully resolved, but it will mark the completion of God's purposes of salvation (9.27, 28).

In 10.1–4 the writer turns on its head the reason that might be given for finding Day of Atonement rituals attractive. The very fact that they are continually offered year after year shows that they are ineffectual in dealing with the consciousness of sin. Instead they provide a constant reminder of sin without the necessary effective means of dealing with it. But Christ's willing bodily obedience means his sacrifice sanctifies and perfects believ-ers once for all time (10.10, 14). Now the writer can return to the concept with which he began this section, that of the new covenant, in order to emphasize in particular its promise – 'I will remember their sins and their lawless deeds no more.' Such a quality of forgiveness removes the reason for any other continuing system of making offering for sins (10.17, 18). Their participation in this new covenant through Christ as mediator means that any problem with continuing sin and a guilty conscience on the part of the addressees is resolved. It remains only for the writer to draw out the implications in an exhortation and a warning. The exhortation is to approach God 'with a true heart in full assurance of faith, with our hearts sprinkled clean from an evil conscience and our bodies washed with pure water' (10.22). The warning is about rejecting the provision that has been made. This would be in effect to trample upon the Son of God and to treat the blood that sealed the new covenant as profane (10.29). In the case of such deliberate apostasy, 'there no longer remains a sacrifice for sins' (10.26). Since Christ's was the final once-for-all sacrifice, there is no alternative means of dealing with the sin of its wilful rejection.

The large-scale enterprise of comparison between the old and the new stages of revelation and their mediators or representatives in the earlier part of the sermon is intended neither to be comparison for its own sake nor exclusively to extol the excellences of the new. Rather, on what seems to be the most convincing construal of the letter's purposes, the stress on the superiority of the Son over the angels, Moses, Joshua, and Aaron and the Levitical priesthood serves the writer's pastoral concern about those who were considering abandoning their distinctive Christological beliefs in order to merge back into what they perceived as the greater security and more tangible benefits of their Jewish heritage. The writer reflects on and expounds both Christ's and believers' relationship to God's earlier revelation in attempting to clarify for his readers what is entailed in their being Jewish *Christians*.

The implications of this identity for the readers' worship and discipleship are further spelled out in two passages at the end of the letter. In the climactic contrast between the two dispensations of revelation in 12.18–24, the readers are reminded that they have not come to the palpable and tangible phenomena associated with the old covenant at Sinai but have come instead to the unseen permanent realities associated with Mount Zion and the heavenly Jerusalem. This access has been made possible by their having come to Jesus, the mediator of a new covenant. The Jewish Scriptures pictured the pilgrimage of the people of God as one from Sinai to Zion, the place of the great covenant assembly of the last days. Now believers are told that in their worship they already participate in this eschatological assembly. God the judge of all is there, but this does not create a sense of terror and fear in the way that God's presence at Sinai is said to have done. This is because Jesus' sprinkled blood speaks a better word than the blood of Abel. Abel's blood cried out from the ground for

justice and vengeance, but Jesus' blood of the new covenant speaks eloquently of God's mercy and grace.

The other passage, which reflects a major purpose of the letter, is
13.9–14. Here the writer claims that, in their worship, believers have a
unique altar – the sacrifice of Christ. Again there is a comparison with
the Jewish sacrificial system, this time as seen in Lev. 16.27, 28, which
legislated the practice of carrying the corpses of sacrificial animals outside
the camp and burning them. Those who did this were involved in defilement and had to purify themselves before being allowed back into the
camp. The writer can now point out that 'Jesus also suffered outside the
city gate', yet, whereas under the Levitical system 'outside' was unsanctified territory, Jesus' death in unsanctified territory is precisely the source
of sanctification. It was 'in order to sanctify the people by his own blood'
(13.12). In this way the readers' notions of clean and unclean, holy and
profane, are further undermined and they can be exhorted to draw the
appropriate implications – 'let us then go to him outside the camp and
bear the abuse he endured' (13.13). They need to be willing to follow
Jesus outside the Jewish religious system, to identify with his marginalization, and to see this move as entailing sanctification rather than defilement, even though it might well invite further abuse, shaming and
persecution. It is a stance that the eschatological convictions that under-
lie their worship should enable them to take. Their participation ahead
of time in the covenant assembly at the heavenly Jerusalem is at the same
time a reminder that 'here we have no lasting city, but we are looking for
the city that is to come' (13.14). Both their access already to the permanence of the heavenly reality and their awareness of the impermanence of
the present order, including its manifestation in the religious system and
values of Judaism, should enable them, while still completing the pilgrimage to the city that is to come, to risk identifying with Jesus and his
suffering outside this system.

Further reading

The introductory sections of some of the major commentaries deal briefly with
occasion and purpose (e.g. Ellingworth 1993: 78–80; deSilva 2000: 16–20;
58–71; Lane 1991: lv–lviii; xcviii–ci).

For variations on the traditional view of the occasion as entailing a return to
Judaism, see Lindars 1991: 4–15 and Gordon 2000: 14–22.

For recent discussions of setting and purpose in sociological terms, see
D. A. deSilva, 'The Epistle to the Hebrews in Social-Scientific Perspective',
Restoration Quarterly 36 (1994), pp. 1–21 and the monographs of Johnson 2001
and Salevao 2002.

6

Use of Jewish Scriptures

The use of Scripture in Hebrews is by no means confined to citing iso-lated texts in support of its argument. It has already become clear in the discussion of this document's genre that it can be seen as a sermon that is based on Scripture and makes extensive use of particular Scrip-tural passages both in its whole composition and in individual sections. As suggested earlier, its sermon can in fact be seen as an implicit midrash woven around Ps. 110.1, 4, the two verses that contain the major theme of Hebrews – the exaltation of Christ at God's right hand (Ps. 110.1) and specifically his exaltation as priest after the order of Melchizedek according to God's oath (Ps. 110.4). As part of the overall exposition of these verses, there are further specific treatments of Scriptural passages and, in the course of their interpretation, these in turn draw in additional Scriptural texts. So, for example, 2.5–18 treats Ps. 8.4–6 and in the process also cites Ps. 22.22 and Isa. 8.17, 18. Hebrews 3.7–4.13 is an exposition based on Ps. 95.7–11 but also brings in Gen. 2.2 and mater-ial from Num. 14. The treatment of Ps. 110.4 in 6.13–7.28 also makes use of Gen. 22.17 and Gen. 14.17–20 and refers to the commandment in Num. 18.21–24. The Scriptural text which forms the basis for the exposition in 8.1–10.18 is Jer. 31.31–34 (cf. 8.8–12) and, as part of that exposition, there is a citation of Exod. 25.40, reference to practices set out in Exod. 30 and Lev. 16, 17, and a citation of Exod. 24.8 and then of Ps. 40.6–8, before a return to the foundational text of Jer. 31.31–34 (cf. 10.16, 17). It was also shown in the earlier discussion in Chapter 2 how Ps. 40.6–8 itself becomes the basis for a similar pattern of exposi-tion in the overlapping section of 10.5–39.

Underlying such use of Scriptural texts is a Christological interpreta-tion that is intent on discovering the meaning of Scripture for the new situation of living in the last days after God's decisive word in the Son has been spoken. This Christological interpretation involves elements of both continuity and discontinuity between the old and the new, and these will be the primary focus of our discussion. Before that, however, some brief comments are required on the text of Scripture and the techniques of interpretation employed in Hebrews.

Text

During the second temple period many diaspora Jews, who had taken on Greek as their primary language, became less familiar with their ancestral language of Hebrew, the language of their Scriptures. The need for translation of the sacred texts into Greek became pressing and this process began in the second half of the third century BCE. The early Christians, whose own writings in Greek now constitute the New Testament, naturally made use of the Greek translations of Scripture available, which have become known as the Septuagint (LXX) and which in places differ somewhat from the Hebrew version of the Jewish Scriptures now known to us. Hebrews, then, employs a LXX text. The two principal witnesses to the LXX are codices A and B. But the text used by Hebrews does not conform exclusively to either of the two. It does, however, usually conform to one or the other, with the majority of its citations following the text of A. In some cases the writer of Hebrews has also introduced minor variations himself in order to adapt the citation to the formulation of his argument. One striking instance in which his scriptural quotation from the LXX differs from the Hebrew version is in 10.5–7, where he cites Ps. 40.6–8. Whereas the Hebrew of the Massoretic text has 'sacrifice and offering you do not desire, but ears you have dug for me', the LXX reads 'sacrifices and offerings you have not desired, but a body you have prepared for me'. Clearly here the LXX rendering allows a Christological interpretation about the definitive offering of the body of Christ as the ultimate sacrifice, which the writer of Hebrews exploits, but which would not have been possible if he had been working from the Hebrew text. The same can be said of the quotation from Hab. 2.3, 4 in 10.37, 38. While the Hebrew Massoretic text has 'coming, it will come', that is, 'it will surely come' and the reference is to the vision that has just been mentioned, the LXX translates this with a masculine participle – 'who is coming, will arrive'. The writer of Hebrews then adds a definite article to the participle and, by so doing, both eliminates any ambiguity in the reference and exploits the possibility of taking this as a reference to Christ, since the Messiah was designated by early Christians as 'the one who is coming' (cf. e.g. Matt. 3.11; 11.3; 21.9; John 1.15, 27; 11.27).

Techniques

Midrashic commentary

In discussing the genre of Hebrews an earlier chapter spoke of the possibility of construing the epistle as a midrashic homily on Ps. 110.1, 4. Such descriptions are somewhat controversial because of the lack of scholarly agreement about what actually constitutes 'midrash' and how applicable that label is to treatments of Scripture within the New Testament. Porton (1981: 62) provides a definition, to which appeal is widely made. He views midrash 'as a type of literature, oral or written, which stands in direct relationship to a fixed, canonical text, considered to be the authoritative and revealed word of God by the midrashist and his audience, and in which this canonical text is explicitly cited or clearly alluded to.' This general definition assumes but does not explicitly state that what stands in relationship to the canonical text is a commentary, usually aimed at applying the text to the argument, questions or setting of the interpreter. Although this type of commentary had its roots in the second temple period, its classical development in the rabbinic midrashim did not begin until the third century CE. For this reason, and because such rabbinic midrashim have a content and flavour that differs significantly from the NT writers' use of their Jewish Scriptures, some scholars object to the term 'midrash' being applied to portions of the New Testament. This seems unduly purist. Provided one is clear that the terms 'midrash' and 'midrashic' are being used to describe an exegetical method or process for commenting on a Scriptural text, in which that text is actually cited or is alluded to at the beginning of the commentary, in which other Scriptural texts are woven into such a commentary, and in which frequently the words of the base text are taken up in the commentary, then in the case of Hebrews, for example, one is speaking of a method that has considerable broad similarities with that of many of the later midrashim. Applying the label in this way need not imply anything further about matters such as genre or attitudes to history. The particularities of any such midrashic treatment of Scripture remain to be investigated in any given case.

Among the more specific techniques of exegesis found in Hebrews as well as in the later rabbinic midrashim is that known as *gezerah shawah*, the establishing of the relationship of two Scriptural texts on the basis of similar wording. So in Heb. 3.7–4.13, Gen. 2.2 can be linked to the base passage from Ps. 95 because the term for 'rest' is found in both texts. In Heb. 5.5, 6 Ps. 2.7 is linked with Ps. 110.4 on the basis of the word 'you'. This is one of the seven rules of interpretation attributed to Rabbi Hillel, as is *qal wahomer*, arguing that what is true in a less important case applies all the more in an important case. This type of exegetical argument contributes to the effectiveness of Hebrews' paraenesis. One example is in 10.28, 29 – 'Anyone who has violated the law of Moses dies without mercy "on the testimony of two or three witnesses". How much worse punishment do you think will be deserved by those who have spurned the Son of God, profaned the blood of the covenant by which they were sanctified, and outraged the Spirit of grace?' Another form of this argument is found in the final vivid contrast between the two forms of revelation in 12.18–29 – 'For if they did not escape when they refused the one who warned them on earth, how much less will we escape if we reject the one who warns from heaven!' (12.25). A further midrashic technique is to string together various Scriptural texts in a *catena* or chain linked by short introductory formulae. Hebrews 1.5–13 with its cluster of seven different texts is a prime example. A further interesting rabbinic principle that is also found in Hebrews is worth mentioning. It is the notion that 'what is not in the Torah is not in the world', the kind of argument from silence that claims that if Scripture does not mention something, it does not exist. Since Genesis makes no mention of Melchizedek's parents, Hebrews can assert that he had no mother or father, no genealogy (7.3).

Typology

The way of treating Scripture that has traditionally been thought to be the most characteristic of Hebrews is typology, which entails seeing patterns of correspondence between earlier and later persons, events, places or institutions. As in the case of drawing analogies, both similarities and differences are crucial in the perceived recurrence of a pattern. Hebrews actually uses the terms 'type' (8.5 – in dependence on Exod. 25.40) and 'antitype' (9.24) but, somewhat confusingly, does so in variance with their modern usage, where the former is the designation for the earlier version and the latter for the later fulfilment. This variance arises from the way in which Hebrews works not only with an earlier–later schema but also with a heaven–earth contrast, in which the real or heavenly can be classified as the type and the earthly copy as the antitype, because the former can be seen as preceding the latter in time. So for Hebrews the heavenly tabernacle is the already existing type and the earthly tabernacle, which was built to correspond to it, is its antitype, sketch or copy.

But Hebrews also contains the way of thinking usually associated with typology, whereby Scripture is seen to provide foreshadowings, partial anticipations of the good things to come, the realities which have now become present in Christ. On the one hand, this typology depends on some basic continuity between the various stages of the same God's working, and yet, on the other, discontinuity is introduced by the way the reality and finality of the antitype is shown to transcend, to be superior to its type. This can be seen, for example, in 3.7–4.13, where the resting place of the land becomes, via a link with God's sabbath rest, a type of the rest of eschatological salvation inaugurated by Christ in God's new 'today' (cf. 3.13, 14). Since the consummation of the rest is still future, there is a continuity because Christian believers need to be exhorted to make every effort to enter the rest, lest they fall through the same sort of disobedience that afflicted the wilderness generation (4.11). But there is also a discontinuity, because such believers can also be said to be already in the process of entering the rest (4.3). The interplay between continuity and discontinuity essential to typology is also what contributes to the effectiveness of the writer's paraenesis. The fulfilment in the antitype raises the stakes for Christian believers. As a result of God's oath, the wilderness generation fell by the sword (cf. Num. 14.43), but Hebrews' addressees face something more fearful than any two-edged sword, the lethal weapon of God's word of judgement, which will expose the intentions of their heart and render them defenceless before the consuming gaze of the one to whom account must be given (4.11–13).

Overall hermeneutical perspectives

The discussion of typology has already moved from mere technique to the issue of overall perspective and to the question of how the continuities and discontinuities between old and new stages of revelation are expressed in Hebrews and are to be explained. These matters will be explored in the rest of this chapter.

Christological reading

In Hebrews it is not just that the old is seen in the light of the new but, more specifically, that Scripture is read in the light of Christ and interpreted in such a way as to show the superiority and finality of what God has done in him. But if this is described as a Christological reading of Scripture, what is meant by 'Christological'? Where does the writer's view of Christ come from? It is not simply a cipher into which he can put any content he wishes. Rather, it is embedded in his early Christian tradition, which already contains interpretation of Jesus' earthly life, his death and exaltation, and his status as God's Son. Writer and readers have an authoritative Scripture in common, but, for the writer, the more significant source of solidarity with his readers is or should be their common confession about Christ. There is a difference between the strength of his hold on and the penetration of his insights into the confession, and those of some of the addressees, and so he uses Scripture as a vital part of his

attempt to bring the readers closer to his own level of understanding and
assurance in regard to the Christological confession.

In some places the writer interprets the Jewish Scriptures Christologically in the traditional sense of a messianic use of texts. An already established messianic tradition of interpretation is taken up, for example,
through the use of Ps. 2.7 and 2 Sam. 7.14 in Heb. 1.5 or through the
extensive use of Ps. 110.1. In others places the writer appears to innovate
– for example, with the use of Ps. 8.4–6 in Heb. 2.6–9. With such messianic readings it is not a matter of proving various convictions about
Christ's person or work from Scripture. These are already assumed as part
of the Christian confession, so that, when the Scripture is read with these
convictions, certain of its features are found to lend themselves to this new
perspective. At the same time, because of the writer's convictions about
Christ as the pre-existent Son and as one with God, he also finds in such
texts that which would never have been said of any human figure, even the
Messiah.

Christological interpretation does not involve simply a one-way
movement from the new to the old. What has already been said about
messianic texts underlines that the writer's Christological confession was
already related to and shaped by the Jewish Scriptures. At the same time,
it is not as if the early Christian confession about Christ that the writer
has inherited is fixed in its formulation, and it is particularly through
bringing it into play with his reading of Scripture that the writer of
Hebrews finds new ways of developing the tradition. Indeed, Hebrews'
central notion of Jesus as the great high priest is precisely an instance of
this. It is a piece of Christological reflection that emerges from thinking
about Jesus in relation to reading Scriptural texts about priesthood, and
thereby enriches the tradition.

The writer's exhortation underlines that the new message the readers
have received about Christ stands in continuity with their heritage. It is the
same God who speaks. So, for example, in 3.1–6 the structure of revelation is depicted as *one* house with God as the builder and Moses as servant
in the house, testifying to the things that were to be spoken later about the
one set over the house as Son. In this way God's speaking in the old order
retains its validity. 'The message declared through angels was valid' (2.2)
and even now can continue to be cited as the oracles of the living God. Yet
this God of Scripture is now also characterized in terms of the divine
actions in Christ and the Spirit. The first citations of Scripture in the
sermon in 1.5–13 are treated as the utterances of God. But then, in 3.7–11,
Ps. 95 is quoted as the direct words of God's Spirit to the readers –
'Therefore, as the Holy Spirit says, "Today, if you hear his voice, do not
harden your hearts as in the rebellion . . ."'. But Scripture can also be seen
as the word of Christ, and one of the most striking illustrations of a

Christological functioning of Scripture is when its texts are in fact placed in the mouth of Christ, as occurs, for example, with Ps. 22.22 and Isa. 8.17, 18 in Heb. 2.12, 13 and with Ps. 40.6–8 in Heb. 10.5–7. So here a Christological reading functions as part of a conviction that the God of Israel is a triune God who speaks through Scripture.

The categories to be discussed in what follows are those that have not only been suggested as characteristic overall hermeneutical perspectives in Hebrews, but also proposed as providing a compelling logic or explanation for the pattern of continuity and discontinuity entailed in its writer's Christological approach to Scripture.

Quotation/retelling

Scripture can be quoted in Hebrews as the oracles of God, Christ or the Spirit, but Eisenbaum (1997: 89–133) has argued that this is part of a pattern at work in the interpretation of Scripture, in which there appears to be a discrimination taking place between speech and narrative. Strikingly, the overwhelming majority of quotations of Scripture all involve some form of direct address and constitute an oracular authoritative word into the present. But Scriptural narrative is hardly ever quoted, and then only briefly or allusively (cf. 4.4; 7.1, 2; 11.5, 21). Instead, Hebrews' main way of dealing with these parts of Scripture is retelling or paraphrasing them. This provides a more distancing effect and also allows more room for the writer's Christian convictions to shape the retelling. In the retold narrative sections the distinctive status of Israel's national institutions and past leaders is downplayed and Scriptural narrative is reoriented to become the preparatory history of the new order and of Christian believers in which, especially in the rehearsal of Israel's history in 11.4–40, its heroes can be seen as Christian marginalized outsiders even before the time of Christ.

Relativization of the old

The Christological reading of Scripture in Hebrews entails some relativizing of the old revelation in the light of the new. This is seen in three main overlapping ways. Scripture points beyond itself by indicating its own inadequacy. This then entails a discontinuity between the old revelation and the new one in Christ, and in the light of the latter the old can now be seen as having been ineffectual.

God's revelation in Scripture can be quoted to show its 'self-confessed inadequacy', as Caird (1959: 47–49) phrased it. Perhaps the clearest example of this phenomenon is in 8.8–13, in which the words of Jer. 31.31–34 are employed to argue that its prophecy of a new covenant obviously entailed that the first one must be deficient in some way, otherwise there would have been no need for a new one. A little earlier, in 7.11, a similar point had been made in connection with Ps. 110.4. Why, the writer asks, does the psalmist speak here of a different priesthood after the order of Melchizedek, if the old Aaronic order was perfectly adequate? Understood in the full light of what God has now done in Christ, Scripture itself attests to the inadequacy of the earlier covenant and its priesthood.

When the old revelation is seen particularly as inscripturated law covenant, the greatest stress on discontinuity emerges. This note is sounded in the theological argumentation that sets out Christ's superiority to the angels, to Moses and to the Aaronic priesthood – the representatives of the law. As 7.11–19 make clear, for Hebrews the law and the priesthood share the same transience, and, since there was clearly meant to be a change in the priesthood, the writer argues, of necessity there must also be a change in the validity and permanence of the law that established it (7.12). So the law, declared by angels (2.2), mediated by faithful Moses (3.2–5), and administered by the Levitical priesthood (7.5–28), is demonstrated to be not only preliminary but also imperfect, inferior to the new revelation in Christ. The strongest language is employed to express the discontinuity in the central theological section of the letter in 8.1–10.18. In 8.6–13, in the contrast between the first and second covenants, the former is said to be deficient and obsolete and ready to vanish away, while in 10.8–10 again in terms of first and second, and this time with special reference to sacrifices, the first – God's will as expressed in the law – is described as abolished in order to establish the second – God's will as embodied in Christ.

In context these texts clearly show that a Christological reading of Scripture does not mean that the old simply leads into the new as a natural extension. In places the new's fulfilment of the old is seen to entail not only that the old's institutions are no longer valid, but also that they never really worked properly at all. Among the reasons given in 7.11–19 for the law's commandment about priesthood having been abrogated is that it was weak and ineffectual and that the law was unable to make anything perfect – and perfection or completion is one of Hebrews' key notions for the eschatological salvation brought by Christ. The argument is elaborated in 9.1–10.18. The first covenant's regulations for worship entailed two tents – a first or outer tent, into which the priests enter continually, and a second, inner tent, into which only the high priest goes. Hebrews draws on the Jewish tradition that the divisions in the tabernacle or temple mirror the division between earth and heaven, the inaccessibility of the holy of holies representing the separateness from earth of God's holy presence in heaven. Yet instead of holding that the cosmic structuring reinforces the validity of these worship arrangements, Hebrews draws a different and radical conclusion about the ineffectiveness of all sacrifices performed in the earthly tents. 'By this the Holy Spirit indicates that the way into the sanctuary has not yet been disclosed as long as the first tent is still standing' (9.8). There was no genuine access to God in heaven, while the old system was still operating.

What then was going on in the offering of such sacrifices? Here Hebrews introduces another outer/inner distinction. The sacrifices and arrangements were temporary 'regulations for the body' (9.10) and purified the flesh (9.13), but they could not 'perfect the conscience of the worshipper' (9.9) or 'purify our conscience from dead works to worship the living God' (9.14). By contrast, Christ's once-for-all sacrifice brings him into the heavenly tent of God's presence (9.11, 12) and reaches the parts of humans other sacrifices cannot reach. A further aspect of this radical conclusion is spelled out in 10.1–4, where the law is said to have 'only a shadow of the good things to come and not the true form of these realities' and so could have no power to deal with sin – 'it is impossible for the blood of bulls and goats to take away sins'. Finally, the innovative Christological reading of Scripture in 10.5–11 makes the same point decisively. Christ is portrayed as quoting Ps. 40.6–8 on coming into the world – 'Sacrifices and offerings you have not desired . . . .' Of course, this critique of sacrifices is not uncommon in the Jewish Scriptures but is never absolute. Yet, with Christ's announcement of this critique and of his coming to do God's will, Hebrews draws a sharp contrast between the two. With the coming of Jesus it is not simply that God does not want sacrifices unless other acts of obedience accompany them or are made primary. Rather, God no longer wants sacrifices at all (cf. 10.8, 9). Instead, the offering of Christ's body is the once-for-all sacrifice for sins (10.10, 12, 14). It is not that sacrifices were never God's will but that, now that Jesus has come, sacrifices, and therefore, by implication, the functioning of the Jerusalem temple, are no longer God's will. It is also not the case that the *significance* of blood sacrifices and priesthood can be left behind as obsolete, but that Christ is now for ever the perfect sacrifice and priest, providing immediate and full access to God's holiness.

In Hebrews, therefore, recognition of the Scriptures as the authoritative word of God is quite compatible not only with their serving as a vehicle for expressing the significance of Christ and the implications of the Christian gospel but also, within this pastoral purpose, for parts of their earlier revelation being seen as superseded by God's final word in Christ and as no longer functioning as regulative norms for the community's worship or ethics.

Distinction between ceremonial and moral law?

It is often thought that the difference Christ makes to the earlier stage of revelation can be summed up in terms of its ceremonial parts being done away with and its moral aspects remaining. In the post-apostolic church this distinction in dealing with the Old Testament was most fully developed by Tertullian (cf. *Pud.* 6.3–5). Initially, it might seem to be appropriate for Hebrews on the assumption that the obsolescence of the first covenant really refers to its ceremonial and cultic aspects, its priesthood and sacrificial system. It should be remembered, however, that this distinction deals only with the use of the law and not other parts of Scripture, and even then it proves to be deficient as an explanation for Hebrews' treatment. It fails to do justice to the fact that for Hebrews, as we have seen, cultic and ceremonial aspects have become antiquated but as part of a larger whole, that of the first covenant and its law. When Hebrews refers to the law, it is to the entire Sinaitic covenant, including its ethical commandments (9.19). What is said about priesthood cannot be separated neatly from ethical issues, because priests offered sacrifices for sins, including transgressions of moral laws. A change in the priesthood entails a change in the law as a whole (7.12); the two share the same transience. And because Jesus is the mediator of a better covenant, the first covenant as a whole is held to have become obsolete and about to disappear (8.6–13).

Promise/law perspective

Since in addition to talking about the law having been changed, Hebrews also employs the language of promise, this raises the question whether it might contain a logic that compares with Paul's promise/law hermeneutic found in Gal. 3 and Rom. 4. In fact, in 6.13–7.27 Hebrews does have its own intriguing version of this promise/law hermeneutic, in which promise is seen to be operative within Scripture both before and after law. As in Paul, the promise is linked with Abraham (6.13, 14 cf. also 11.8–19). But, as has been seen in the earlier treatment of this passage, Hebrews adds to its reference to promise the notion of God's oath from Gen. 22.16. This treatment of Abraham prepares for a return to Ps. 110.4, the earlier citation of which has already featured God's oath. Accordingly, Heb. 6.18 goes on to speak of two unchangeable realities, in which it is impossible that God should prove false – the divine promise and oath. Understanding Scripture in the light of what has happened in Christ, the writer can argue that Christian believers also have these realities. The form in which they have them, as 6.19, 20 make clear, is in the exaltation of Jesus on their behalf to heaven and his presence there as a high priest for ever after the order of Melchizedek. This point is made explicitly a little later – in 7.20–22. In the better hope of the new covenant promise its high priest was addressed with an oath – 'The Lord has sworn and will not change his mind, "You are a priest forever".' God has gone on oath and Jesus as high priest is the embodiment of that oath. Now the law came later than the promise-oath to Abraham – at the time of the Levitical priesthood (7.11a) – but the law does not supersede the promise-oath, because there would have been no need for a second promise-oath about a priest according to the order of Melchizedek if the law was meant to be permanent or if it was effectual (cf. 7.11b, 18). As 7.28 asserts – 'For the law appoints as high priests those who are subject to weakness, but the word of the oath, which came later than the law, appoints a Son who has been made perfect forever.' But this creative Christological reading has more to offer when the Genesis 14 account of Abraham and Melchizedek is brought into the picture. Abraham's action of giving tithes to Melchizedek is viewed as representing his descendants, including Levi, who were thereby recognizing the superiority of the Melchizedek priesthood and the inferiority of the law, its priesthood and its tithing regulations (cf. 7.7–10). Melchizedek, by blessing Abraham who had received the promise, confirms that promise, and, at the same time, by collecting tithes from Abraham, relativizes the law even before it was actually given (cf. 7.6).

This passage provides a striking illustration of a promise/law hermeneutic operating more generally in Hebrews. This hermeneutic serves the theological point that the law is now to be seen as ineffectual in dealing with humanity's sin, and that, with the certainty and immutability of the fulfilment of the promise-oath in Christ, God takes full and decisive responsibility for dealing with that sin once and for all.

Theological exposition/paraenesis

As a general rule, as Hughes (1979: 54–73) in particular has pointed out, there appears to be more of an emphasis on continuity in the sections of paraenesis and more of an emphasis on discontinuity in the sections of theological exposition. Discontinuity is to the fore in the exposition of the comparison between God's word in Christ and the Mosaic law and covenant. But continuity is stronger in the exhortations. So the paraenesis of 3.7–4.13 is a midrashic application of Ps. 95 to the lives of the addressees. The exhortation to endurance and faithfulness in 10.36–39 makes direct use of the words of Hab. 2.3, 4. And throughout 11.4–40 the faith of figures from the Jewish Scriptures is treated as a model for Christian believers. Then, in 12.5, 6, such believers can again be addressed directly by the exhortation of Prov. 3.11, 12 – 'My child, do not regard lightly the discipline of the Lord . . .'. But in all such exhortation it is not as if the readers are simply thought of as in precisely the same situation as their earlier counterparts. Their new situation as believers in Christ is assumed and it is the combination of the text with this situation which gives rise to a new form of the word of God that addresses them. This can be seen in the way the LXX wording of Ps. 8 can be exploited to fit the situation of Christian believers in 2.6–9, in the way the resting place of the land in 3.7–4.13 becomes the eschatological rest of salvation, into which believers already enter, or in the way it can be said of Moses in the creative anachronism of 11.26 that 'he considered abuse suffered for the Christ to be greater wealth than the treasures of Egypt'. The underlying assumption about the new situation that makes possible this use of Scripture is in fact spelled out in 11.39, 40 – 'all these, though they were commended for their faith, did not receive what was promised, since God had provided something better so that they would not, apart from us, be made perfect'.

The already/not yet of eschatology

The tension between God's earlier revelation in some places continuing to provide God's word to the Christian community and yet in others being dismissed as obsolete can also be seen to reflect the writer's eschatology, as again Hughes (1979: 66–70) has persuasively shown. In other words, one of the filters that determines for the writer how much continuity and how much discontinuity there will be as the Jewish Scriptures function for Christian believers is his experience of the end-times, his belief about what has happened in the Son in these last days. In the theological sections with their Christological focus the writer is stressing the 'already' of what God has done in Christ, the finality of its fulfilment of the old, its embodiment of permanent heavenly reality. Here the earlier revelation is seen to be most relativized and outmoded by its own culmination. Yet the end has not fully come and believers have to press on to the ultimate eschatological goal. Here the writer finds the closest continuity with the older revelation. Scriptural exhortations to faith, perseverance and endurance can still apply or be updated, as can their promises and threats of judgement, while believers' 'not yet' continues. So it is not only a relation between the present and the past that is operative in a Christological reading of Scripture but also a relationship between both of these and the future.

The language of promise from Scripture comes into play again here (with the promise to Abraham, the promise of rest and a city to come, the promise of a new covenant) and with it the notion of promise and fulfilment. Indeed, the whole of Scripture can be seen as promise. The opening statement that in the past God spoke through the prophets is not to be interpreted narrowly. In fact, of the thirty-one Scriptural passages that may actually be cited in Hebrews, seven are from the Prophets, twelve from the Pentateuch and twelve from the Writings (eleven from Psalms, and one from Proverbs). This suggests that, for Hebrews, all of Scripture is being viewed as prophetic. Its promises witness to a future beyond its own boundaries and the future of those promises then has two stages in the last days – present fulfilment and future consummation. Which of these two stages is in view determines the writer's choice and use of Scriptural texts for his argument.

What has emerged from the above discussion is that the writer's Christological key to interpretation produces a number of different patterns of coherence in the reading of Scripture. No one formulation of their logic, even a necessarily nuanced one, adequately captures the diversity and dynamism of the moves between old and new generated by such a reading.

Further reading

On the actual citations in Hebrews, see K. J. Thomas, 'The Old Testament Citations in Hebrews', *NTS* 11 (1964–65), pp. 303–25.

For a good general discussion of the writer's exegetical methodology, see G. B. Caird, 'The Exegetical Method of the Epistle to the Hebrews', *CJT* (1959), pp. 44–51.

For a more extensive discussion of midrash, see G. Porton, 'Defining Midrash', in J. Neusner (ed.), *The Study of Ancient Judaism* (New York: Ktav, 1981), pp. 55–92.

The most helpful monograph on the writer's overall hermeneutical perspective remains that of Hughes 1979.

7

Christ, Salvation, Eschatology and Christian Existence

The previous chapters on the writer's rhetoric, the flow of his argument, the purposes of his writing and his use of the Scriptures have already enabled an appreciation of how he develops and applies his theology as a preacher and pastor. In this chapter more systematic consideration will be given to four major areas of thought that emerge from his theologizing. If its perspectives on these areas are to be adequately understood, the presuppositions about God and humanity, with which its writer operated and which are often remote from present-day readers, need to be explored briefly.

Presuppositions of the theology of Hebrews

Both the exposition and the exhortation sections of the epistle are pervaded by assumptions, inherited from the Jewish Scriptures and Jewish cultic practices, about holiness, sin, and atonement, and these shape the way in which both God and humans are viewed. Holiness has to do with the basic distinction between God as Creator and God's creation. It signifies the incomparable otherness of God. At the same time this wholly different God wills to be in relationship with human creatures and wills that Israel in particular should somehow reflect God's holiness in its relationship to the nations by being a holy people ('You shall be holy, for I the Lord your God am holy' – Lev. 19.2). In willing the good and in willing life, God wills that all of human life should be lived in an orderly fashion. The Jewish Scriptures reflect the view that a life-threatening disorder has, however, disrupted the good order established by God at creation. Such disorder was expressed in a number of ways – as a chaos invading creation on a grand scale, as a contagion that affected physical life, and as moral contamination. Leviticus, on which Hebrews draws extensively, focuses especially on worship as the heart of God's relationship with Israel and as the sphere in which an order which will affect the whole of life is to be established. The place in which God's presence was held to be especially manifested and available – the tabernacle and its holy of holies – has therefore to be kept free from the threat of disorder. Access to the presence of the holy God has to be properly managed, human impurity has to be dealt with, and in the process appropriate distinctions between what is holy and profane, what is clean and unclean, have to be made. Mixing categories, with the accompanying improper exchange of matters belonging to different spheres, not only brings disorder but can drive God from the sanctuary.

The notion of sin included this sort of impurity, which could occur simply in the course of everyday living, and moral transgressions, which were also a feature of Israel's life. However, God was seen as making provision for dealing with all forms of uncleanness through the sacrificial system, which culminated in the rituals of the Day of Atonement. 'For on this day atonement shall be made for you, to cleanse you; from all your sins you shall be clean before the Lord' (Lev. 16.30). In the centre of this day's rituals was the mercy seat over which God's presence was manifested and which had to be sprinkled with the blood of sacrificial animals if atonement for sin was to be made. The terms 'atonement' and 'mercy seat' are both cognates of a verb meaning 'to cover' (*kipper*) and signal that Israel's uncleanness had to be covered if a holy God was to dwell among the people. In the process both the threat to the profanation of God's name through Israel acting in ways that were incongruous with God's character and the threat to the community through pollution were taken care of, God's presence in the sanctuary could once again be counted on, and a relationship to this God that had become distorted could be rehabilitated. The cultic arrangements make possible and mediate the presence of God in the midst of Israel.

Priests are part of this mediating process, needing first to be made holy so that they can represent God's purity and then can guarantee the proper order that will keep impurity at bay. Priests offer sacrifices for the people, the means for restoring impure humans to a relationship with their holy God. To this end, various types of sacrifice are brought by the people. Two particular forms of gifts and sacrifices are established in Leviticus 4–5. The 'sin offering' enables purification by dealing with the stain that particular acts can bring on a person, while the 'guilt offering' enables restitution by dealing with the guilt and indebtedness caused by sin, which would render the transgressor liable to punishment (cf. Lev. 5.17).

Blood and death play an important role in this system of holiness. On the one hand, contact with death in a variety of forms, and especially with corpses, pollutes; and blood, when lost in violent death or in menstruation, defiles. On the other hand, sacrifices are the means of the restoration of holiness and these sacrifices paradoxically involve blood and death. Indeed, the blood of the sacrificial victim stands for life taken violently through death. 'It is the blood that makes atonement' (Lev. 17.11). In this way sacrificial blood becomes the means of transition from the sphere of the unholy to the sphere of the holy, and the smoke rising from the burnt offerings of the sacrifices can be seen to represent the passage from the seen to the unseen world, from the earthly to the heavenly.

If the world of Leviticus seems alien to modern sensibilities, Brueggemann (1997: 191–92) warns against simply dismissing it as primitive and sees different sorts of threats, such as that posed by the toxic contamination from nuclear waste, as analogues in our world. Those who lived through the foot and mouth disaster in the UK in 2001 also experienced something analogous to ancient Israel's experience of life-threatening impurity. The virus that spread impurity through herds of cattle and flocks of sheep threatened the livelihood of whole communities and the slaughter of thousands of animals was seen as a necessity to keep it at bay. The countryside was marred by the sight of smoke rising from holocausts of animals in an attempt to stop the spread of contagion and to restore order and health to rural life. The threat from impurity was further brought home by the rituals of disinfecting, which the public had to perform on entering and leaving affected areas.

The categories from Leviticus and the sense of reality they represent provide a way into the world of Hebrews and its perspective on Christ's person and work. In its worldview the holy God remains sovereign, awesome and terrifying. 'Our God is a consuming fire' who is to be worshipped with reverence and awe (12.28, 29). This recalls the depiction of God both at Sinai – 'Now the appearance of the glory of the Lord was like a devouring fire on the top of the mountain' (Exod. 24.17) – and before the entry into the land: 'For the Lord your God is a devouring fire, a jealous God' (Deut. 4.24). The author of Hebrews also speaks in 10.26–31 of what awaits those who, having received the truth, wilfully persist in sin. There is 'a fearful prospect of judgement, and a fury of fire that will consume the adversaries', because 'it is a fearful thing to fall into the hands of the living God'. This holy God continues to insist that worshippers be holy, and Hebrews speaks of 'the holiness without which no one will see the Lord' (12.14). It is only when such a God has made the appropriate provision for humans to be in the divine presence that such a presence no longer consumes and judges. That provision makes humans holy, purges, perfects and sanctifies them by delivering them from the guilt and power of sin and from the death that is sin's consequence. For Hebrews God's provision is now embodied in a person and, if the necessary holiness and perfection of humanity is to be achieved, this agent of salvation needs to be identified with the holy God but also identified with humanity in a way that somehow shares its condition without being personally tainted by it, and that at the same time is able to change that condition.

Christology

This means that the key concept, though by no means the dominant title, for the writer's Christology is that of mediator. Christ is the figure who bridges the apparently incommensurable gap between a holy God and unholy creatures. This also explains why what initially seem to be two quite different ways of depicting Christ sit side by side in this epistle. It starts out by asserting that Christ is 'the reflection of God's glory and the exact imprint of God's very being, and he sustains all things by his powerful word' (1.3) and yet later can say of this same person that he is a fully human being, who is like other humans in every respect (2.17), so much so that he 'offered up prayers and supplications, with loud cries and tears' and 'learned obedience through what he suffered' (5.7, 8). For Hebrews these are not two independent Christological traditions that have been loosely combined. Both aspects of this portrayal have to be held together and taken equally seriously if the true nature of Christ as intermediary is to be appreciated. The actual designation of Christ as mediator occurs three times in the argument (8.6; 9.15; 12.24), and each time this is with reference to the new covenant, the new and better arrangement for the relationship between God and God's people, which the writer holds to have been inaugurated through God's activity in Christ. It is noticeable that it is both Christ's person and his work that make him the mediator of the new covenant. The first reference in 8.6 comes after it has been established that Christ as God's Son is a permanent high priest after the order of Melchizedek, one who has been exalted to heaven (cf. 7.28; 8.1), and the second in 9.15 comes after it has been asserted that his offering of himself is able to achieve what the offering of animal sacrifices could not achieve (cf. 9.14). The final reference occurs in the climactic contrast between the old and new dispensations in 12.18–24, and brings both aspects together. Believers are able to participate in the worship of the heavenly Zion because they come 'to Jesus, the mediator of a new covenant, and to the sprinkled blood that speaks a better word than the blood of Abel' (12.24).

These explicit references to Christ as mediator are already associated with his role as Son and high priest, which are the two key titles for the writer's argument. But before pursuing these more fully, it is worth continuing reflection on the structure of the relationship between a transcendent, holy God and sinful human beings, which the writer presupposes. From the Jewish Scriptures it is clear that, for such a God to be in relation to creatures, intermediaries have always been necessary. The entire rhetorical structure of the writer's argument with its *synkrisis*, the comparison between the old and the new, depends on this notion. The comparison and contrast is between a variety of earlier forms of mediation (God's speech through the prophets, angels, Moses, the

Levitical priesthood) and a final and decisive mediation in Christ. Mediation language is also explicitly employed of God's speech in 6.17, where a literal translation would be: 'he mediated or intervened (NRSV – guaranteed it) with an oath'.

It is the notion of mediation through God's word that in fact informs the two key titles for the argument of the sermon – Son and high priest. These are not treated totally distinctly. Rather, both combine to enable the writer to make his point effectively. That point is that God has spoken in a final and decisive way in a particular person, Jesus Christ, and the message of salvation is not to be rejected unless the audience are willing to incur the direst consequences. Both the Son and the high priest are forms of God's speech. God has spoken in the Son, and God has sworn an oath in the high priest. These two titles, as has been noted earlier, are also linked through the use of Ps. 110. Psalm 110.1, read in the light of Ps. 2.7 (cf. 1.5), establishes Jesus as the exalted Son, and Ps. 110.4 establishes him as the high priest. In addition, it is through his obedience and suffering as the Son in his earthly ministry that Jesus is qualified to become the heavenly high priest. While sonship language for Christ is to the fore in the first part of Hebrews in 1.1–5.10, the imagery of high priest for Christ is to the fore in the long middle section of the letter from 7.1–10.25, but the two titles and roles are brought together in 4.14, 15; 5.5, 6; 5.8–10; 7.3; 7.28.

The significance of the language about the Son in 1.1–4 and the movement of thought it entails should be noted. The Son, who is the embodiment of God's mediating word, representing God's immanence within created history, is at his exaltation appointed heir of all things, of the cosmos. But this Word embodied in the Son had a role in creation and an essential relation to God prior to creation. This formulation takes up Wisdom imagery, in which Wisdom existed at the beginning before the creation of the world, was at God's side and was instrumental in creation (cf. Prov. 8.22–31; Wis. 9.1, 2), and Wisdom and the Logos or Word were often treated as functional equivalents in Hellenistic Jewish thought (cf. Wis. 9.1, 2; Philo, *Fug.* 97, 108–9; *Somn.* 2.242, 245). Hebrews' pattern of thought continues the Wisdom motif, applied to the Son, by moving forward again to the Son's present role in sustaining creation, and then focuses on his earthly mission with its work of purification and its culmination in his exaltation to God's right hand, thereby concluding where it had begun. In the process vv. 2c, 3a place the Son on the side of the Creator rather than the creatures, and this emphasis will be continued in the discussion of the Son's superiority to angels in 1.5–13, esp. vv. 8, 10–12. Without explaining it or even making it explicit, this pattern of thought has presupposed that the uncreated, pre-existent, eternal Son became human in an incarnation.

This thought is developed, however, in 2.5–18, which does not employ the title 'Son' but makes plain that the one who for a little while was made lower than the angels is the same Son who has been described as superior to the angels, and that the Jesus who is exalted is the same figure as the Son whose exaltation has just been celebrated (cf. 2.9). In addition, the argument will return to explicit use of 'Son' language in 3.6, when it takes up Christ's quality of faithfulness, which has been introduced in 2.5–18. Through the use of Ps. 8 this passage depicts the Son as the representative human being, through whom the destiny of humanity as a whole is fulfilled. The formulations of vv. 14, 17 about sharing the flesh and blood of human beings and needing to become like them in every respect imply, of course, that there was a previous mode of existence of the Son in which he did not share flesh and blood, and therefore again also imply an incarnation. As Son, Jesus mediates between God and humanity, and it is only because of such an identity that he is able to taste death for everyone in a way that removes death's sting (cf. 2.14) and to make a sacrifice of atonement that is an effective one.

It is at the close of the argument of 2.5–18 that the title 'high priest' is first employed for Christ (cf. v. 17). Because the Son has become fully human, he is able to help Abraham's descendants and serve as their high priest. The sequence of thought signals that, for the writer, the common early Christian belief in Jesus as the Son of God is foundational for his own more innovative portrayal of Jesus as high priest. When the qualifications of Jesus for high priesthood are elaborated in 4.14–5.10, the emphasis is similar. The Son of God who has been exalted to the heavenly realm as high priest is able to perform this role on behalf of humans because his earthly obedience and suffering mean that he is in full solidarity with humans and their weakness. When deeper teaching on Christ as high priest according to the order of Melchizedek is offered in 6.13–7.28, the stress falls on this priesthood being for ever, as Christ's eternal status as Son of God (cf. 7.3), his indestructible life (cf. 7.16) and the permanent availability of his priestly presence (cf. 7.24) feature in the exposition. In 8.1–10.18 the focus shifts from the person of the high priest to his work, but the efficacy of that work and his ability to function as mediator between a holy God and an unholy humanity continues to depend on the divine Son being fully human and yet without sin. This high priest offers himself as a sacrifice that is without blemish (9.14), and this takes up the earlier emphasis that Christ as high priest is 'without sin' (cf. 4.15) and 'holy, blameless, undefiled, separated from sinners' (7.26).

It is sometimes asked when Hebrews envisages Christ as becoming high priest. Is it only when he enters the heavenly sanctuary, or is he already depicted as a high priest on earth and particularly in his death? Hebrews' concern is, however, far more with his present status and role than with pinpointing precisely when this came into effect. If the question is pressed, then perhaps it is best to consider the likely development of the writer's thought about Jesus as a high priest according to the order of Melchizedek. The writer would have shared with other early Christians the notion that the address to the king and priest of Ps. 110 had become applicable to Jesus as a result of his exaltation to heaven. But once he develops Jesus' priesthood so that this includes Jesus' offering of himself as a sacrifice, that priesthood is not restricted, as in 9.11, 12, to the imagery of the exalted Jesus entering heaven with the sacrifice he had previously made on earth. Rather, Jesus' final act in death is drawn into the significance of his exaltation so that both are encompassed in his priestly work – 'But when Christ had offered for all time a single sacrifice for sins, "he sat down at the right hand of God"' (10.12; cf. also 2.17). Christ's priesthood was operative on both the earthly and the heavenly levels. The notion of heavenly priesthood also casts its light back on the rest of Jesus' earthly life, the nature of which is seen as constituting his qualification for priesthood (cf. 2.17, 18; 4.15; 5.7–10). Indeed, just as the title 'Son' is pushed back from the resurrection and exaltation to the sphere of pre-existence (1.2), so there is also a sense in which the Melchizedek priesthood of Jesus, when associated with 'Son of God', is seen as eternal in nature, 'having neither beginning of days nor end of life' (7.3).

This trajectory for the image of Christ as priest prompts the reflection that, starting from the belief in Christ's exaltation, Hebrews has an implied narrative of his role. This starts with his pre-existence (1.2), moves to his coming into the world in solidarity with humanity (1.6; 2.14a; 10.5) and progresses through his mission of redemption, beginning in his earthly life of testing, obedience and suffering (2.10, 18; 4.15; 5.8), culminating in his sacrificial death on the cross (1.3b; 2.17b; 9.26; 12.2), and climaxing in his exaltation to heaven (1.3b; 4.14; 8.1; 9.12; 10.12; 12.2). In heaven Christ intercedes for those who approach him by faith (4.16; 7.25) and he will appear from heaven at the end of history to appropriate his inheritance, defeat finally all enemies and complete the work of salvation (1.2b; 9.28; 10.13, 37).

But Hebrews' story of Christ is not simply that of an individual who acts on behalf of humanity; he also acts as representative of humanity. Its writer employs two other significant and distinctive titles for Christ that underline this aspect of his identity – 'pioneer' (2.10; 12.2) and 'forerunner' (6.20). These depict Jesus as a heroic representative figure who blazes the trail of faith and salvation into the heavenly realm for those with whom he shares flesh and blood. In solidarity with him, humans can follow the new and living way of full access into the presence of God that he has inaugurated (cf. also 10.20). Associated with the 'pioneer' description is another distinctive notion that Hebrews applies to Christ's life, that of its perfecting (2.10; 5.9; 7.28). Previous to the incarnation in Jesus, the Son always already existed (1.2b, 3a). Nevertheless Jesus also receives the name of Son at his exaltation (cf. 1.4, 5). For Hebrews both perspectives hold, because it is through his earthly life that Jesus becomes perfected or completed as the Son – 'although he was a Son, he learned obedience through what he suffered' (5.8). Through the obedience of suffering and death, the incarnate Son experienced that which the pre-existent Son could never experience. His lifelong obedience culminated in the perfect offering of himself in death to God. In this way, 'having been made perfect, he became the source of eternal salvation' for other humans (5.9) or 'the perfecter of our faith' (12.2).

The perfecting of Jesus' humanity took place over the course of his lifetime and as part of a process that involved conflict and struggle with the sinful conditions of its existence. This entails that the humanity assumed by the pre-existent Son was not an already perfect humanity but one that suffered from the effects of sin. Although it was without sin, it felt the force of temptation, was susceptible to death, and was fearful in the face of death (cf. 2.14, 15; 4.15; 5.7). The union of the pre-existent Son and the human Jesus was the means of the perfecting of his humanity, and the goal of the earthly mission of this Son was the perfection of humanity as a whole. A perfected humanity, then, is the result of the divine becoming one with the human. Unless Jesus were both, his human obedience and death would not be saving, his own perfected humanity would not be the source of perfection for others. This returns us to the concept of mediation with which we began the discussion of Christology. In two places Hebrews describes its perspective on Christ as pioneer or as high priest as 'fitting' (2.10; 7.26). Given the worldview Hebrews presupposes, with its estrangement between a holy God and unholy creatures, it is indeed fitting that the one who mediates salvation as perfection be both fully in solidarity with humans, sharing their sufferings, and yet at the same time fully in solidarity with divine holiness and separate from actual sin.

Soteriology

The broad term 'salvation' does feature in Hebrews as a description of that which is mediated from God to humanity by Christ. The noun 'salvation' occurs in 1.14; 2.3, 10; 5.9; 6.9; 9.28 and the verb 'to save' is found in 7.25. Human experience of this divine rescue act or deliverance has a future orientation, since salvation is seen as being fully received or inherited at the end of history (cf. 1.14; 2.10; 9.28). At the same time this deliverance is also a present and continuing experience on the basis of a past action of God in Christ (cf. 2.3, 4, 10; 5.9; 7.25). The eschatological dimensions of salvation will be explored more fully in the next section of this chapter, but here it should be noted that the distinctive language of perfecting, which was used of Christ, is also a dominant category for the salvation he accomplishes and again clearly gives salvation a future orientation. The divine rescue act is seen as one that brings God's purposes for humanity to completion. What the law and its sacrifices were unable to achieve, Christ brought to realization through his sacrifice, which perfected believers for all time by overcoming sin and death and which continues to bring them into the consummation and completion of their relationship to God (cf. 6.1; 7.11, 19; 9.9; 10.1, 14; 11.40; 12.23; 13.21).

The focus of this section will, however, be on the main ways in which the salvation Christ has already achieved is depicted. Elsewhere in the New Testament some of the primary images for salvation are drawn from the law court (with the language of judgement, righteousness and justification), from the Jewish cult (with the language of sacrifice and atonement), from the sphere of relationships (with the language of reconciliation), from the slave market (with the language of redemption) and from battle (with the language of the defeat of or victory over hostile powers). The forensic language of accountability to the divine judge and of being approved as righteous is by no means absent from Hebrews (cf. 4.12, 13; 6.2; 10.27, 30; 11.4, 7; 12.23). The *Christus Victor* motif, in which Christ conquers the devil, is combined with talk of freedom from the plight of slavery in 2.14, 15, and 'redemption' terminology occurs in 9.12, 15, where the implicit slavery in view is servitude to transgression of the law. But, given again that the predominant view of the human plight in Hebrews is that of the gulf between an unholy humanity and a holy God, it is no surprise that the pervasive imagery for salvation is drawn from the cult and that this draws into its orbit both the notion of redemption (cf. 9.12, 15) and the concept of the restoration of a personal relationship, formulated elsewhere, for example in the language of reconciliation in the Pauline writings.

Since the human situation is viewed in terms of impurity and taint, caused by sin and guilt, and these are regarded as impeding access to the holy and as blighting human integrity, Christ's death, which provides the solution, is depicted as a sacrifice and an atonement. In particular, the significance of that death is expounded in terms of the Day of Atonement ritual, discussed earlier in the section on the presuppositions of Hebrews' theology. The work of Jesus as high priest is described as making 'a sacrifice of atonement for the sins of the people' (2.17) and the analogy between his offering and that of the Aaronic high priest on the Day of Atonement is developed especially in 9.6–14. Atonement primarily entails expiation, the restoring of a relationship through removal of the sin that had disrupted it (cf. 9.26b; also 10.11, 12). But just as atonement in the Jewish Scriptures could also involve propitiation, the dealing with sin in order to avert the wrath of God (cf. e.g. Num. 16.46), so also in Hebrews it has this secondary connotation, since the divine wrath is emphasized (cf. 3.10, 11, 17; 4.3) and Christ's sacrifice is seen as dealing with God's furious and fiery judgement (10.26–31). The importance of sacrificial blood and death within the Jewish cultic system has already been noted. Hebrews continues to emphasize this means of transition from the sphere of the unholy to that of the holy in its depiction of Christ's sacrifice. This high priest offers not the blood of animals but his own blood, the symbol of his life taken in violent death (9.12–14). His inauguration of the new covenant, just like that of the old, requires a blood sacrifice, for 'without the shedding of blood there is no forgiveness of sins' (9.15–22; cf. 10.19, 29; 12.24; 13.12). The superiority of Christ's sacrifice lies in his not having to make any offering for himself and in his voluntary offering of his own body in death and in the very presence of God (9.24–26; 10.5–10). The difference between an offering high priest and an offered victim is collapsed into the notion of self-sacrifice, since Jesus as high priest offers himself as willing victim. What is more, this sacrifice does not have to be repeated, but is decisive and final. It is once for all (*ephapax* – 7.27; 9.12, 26; 10.10) and effective for all time (7.25; 10.12, 14). Here it must be remembered that the person and the work of Christ cannot be separated. It is because this high priest is one with God as well as one with humans that his sacrifice of himself has this quality of finality and participates in the permanent and eternal validity that belongs to the divine sphere.

The imagery of atoning sacrifice with reference to Christ's death overlaps with the categories of purification and sanctification, since all have in view dealing with the sin that defiles humans and prevents them from entering the presence of a holy God. Salvation is viewed as purification in Hebrews (1.3; 9.22), and in particular it is the human conscience that is purged or cleansed in order to be able to worship the living God (9.13, 14; cf. also 10.2, 22). Salvation by means of Christ's death is also depicted as sanctification, a setting apart for a holy God that is at the same time a setting apart from what is unholy (2.11; 9.13; 10.10, 14, 29; 13.12). In the Jewish sacrificial cult blood and death were defiling, but also paradoxically the means of restoring holiness. The paradox is maintained and intensified in Hebrews, especially when in 13.11–13 Jesus' sacrifice outside the city gates is likened to the destruction of the bodies of the sacrificial animals outside the camp in the place of defilement. His death in the place of apparent defilement is precisely the means of sanctification for the people by his blood.

Just as the issue of access to the presence of a holy God in the sanctuary in the midst of Israel was at the heart of the rationale for the Jewish cult, so qualification for access to a holy God is the goal of salvation as perfection, atonement, purification and sanctification in Hebrews. It is striking that the exhortation that follows the long central section of exposition about Christ's sacrificial death urges the hearers to approach in worship with full assurance of faith, since the blood of Jesus has opened access to the heavenly sanctuary of God's presence (10.19–22). It is also no accident that the *peroratio* sounds the same note. Believers have approached in worship the heavenly Zion, where they are in the presence of God the judge and Jesus the mediator (12.22–24), and they are now able to offer worship or service that is pleasing to God (12.28).

This discussion of Christ's death as an unrepeatable, once-for-all sacrifice should not be taken to mean that salvation in Hebrews is a backward-looking phenomenon. The use of the sacrificial metaphor within an eschatological framework provides an emphatic reminder that until the consummation sin remains a problem to be dealt with even within the new order that has been inaugurated. For Hebrews the exalted Christ makes his once-for-all sacrifice continually available and effective through his living presence before God as high priest. In Christ's role as both sacrificial victim and high priest for ever his death and resurrection are both presupposed. His death entails the restoration of relationship with a holy God and his resurrection and exaltation mean that the restored relationship is also something radically new, a new and better covenant based on the power of Christ's indestructible life and introducing a better hope (7.15–22).

Eschatology

Talk of hope leads into this letter's vision for the future. The issues that have dominated discussion of eschatology in Hebrews are how its temporal and spatial aspects are to be related, and whether its writer's particular mix of these categories remains within the frame of thought found in apocalyptic writings or needs to be explained in relation to the worldview of Philo or of middle Platonism. These broad issues entail a variety of more specific questions. Is the emphasis in Hebrews' perspective on the future simply on the permanence and unchangeableness of the heavenly world? What has happened to the eschatological notion of a new heaven and new earth in Hebrews? Does final salvation remain in the permanent heavenly sphere, or do expressions such as the age to come and the city to come retain both temporal and spatial connotations? Does a temporal or a spatial dualism, whatever the origin of the latter, predominate, or are the two held together in a coherent fashion, or is there simply an unresolved tension in the writer's thought?

What are the data that provoke such questions? The *exordium* of 1.1–4 is imbued with an eschatological perspective and it is one that conforms fully to what would be expected of an early Christian adaptation of Jewish hopes. God's speaking in the Son is said to have taken place 'in these last days' (literally, 'at the end of these days'), thereby decisively inaugurating the final stage of history and ushering in the age to come. But the Son is also the one through whom God originally created 'the ages' (NRSV – 'the universe'; cf. also 11.3). The term 'age' (*aiōn*) had both temporal and spatial connotations. The LXX frequently used this term to translate the Hebrew *'olam*, which had a dual reference either to 'age' or 'world', and so this Greek equivalent also became pressed into double service. In its sense of 'time or duration of the world' it could easily serve as a reference to the world itself and so became a synonym for *kosmos*. In 1 Cor. 1.20; 2.6; 3.18, 19 Paul employs these two Greek terms virtually interchangeably. 'Age' could stand, therefore, for a period of the world seen in its cosmic scope of heaven and earth, and in apocalyptic literature both 'this age' and 'the age to come' included the two strands of the created universe – heaven and earth. Here in Hebrews Christ is not only said to be the one through whom these came into being but also the one who is the heir of 'all things', a further way of designating the total cosmos. His eschatological inheritance will include the whole created universe. The *exordium* also follows other early Christian thinking in holding that in the time between the inauguration of the last days and the consummation of all things the centre of gravity for believers is where Christ now is in the heavenly realm – 'he sat down at the right hand of the Majesty on high'. This traditional Christian modification of Jewish eschatological expectations at the outset of Hebrews would lead one to expect that any emphasis on heaven in the rest of the argument would primarily serve this framework, in which a focus on the 'already' aspect of eschatological salvation frequently came to expression through reference to heaven, to Christ's present rule from there and to believers' links to Christ in that realm.

Jewish and early Christian usage of the terms 'heaven' and 'the heavens' was a fluid one with a variety of references. These terms could refer to either the upper part of the created universe or to the uncreated realm of God, because this upper part was seen as pointing beyond itself to the divine transcendence. Even within its usage for the created heavens there was a dual function, first to refer to the sky or cosmic heavens and then to speak of the created but invisible spiritual world inhabited by angelic powers, which the upper limits of the cosmos were held to conceal. To complicate matters further, sometimes one of these references is in view but at other times two of them are combined, whether in regard to both parts of the created heavens, visible and invisible, or to both the invisible spiritual realm and the divine abode to which it points. Hebrews also follows this pattern of usage. In 1.10–12 the earth and the heavens are the created universe. They are perishable, will be rolled up and changed, and this in contrast to Christ who created them and remains the same. Similarly, according to 12.26, 27, there will be a future final shaking of earth and heaven, both parts of the created realm, in order that what cannot be shaken – God's kingdom – will remain. What is not explicit here, however, is what the relation of that kingdom to the created world will be after the final shake-up. In the meantime Christ can be said to have passed through the created heavens (4.14), to be exalted above these heavens (7.26) and to have entered into the inner shrine of the divine sanctuary (6.19), where he is seated at the right hand of the throne of the Majesty in the heavens (8.1). In the words of 9.24 – 'he entered into heaven itself, now to appear in the presence of God on our behalf'.

Because of Christ's work and through their relation to Christ, believers on earth already have access to the realm of heaven and to God's presence (4.16; 10.19, 20). In a reference that combines the created spiritual realm and the abode of God, they can be said to have come to the heavenly Jerusalem, to innumerable angels, to the assembly of the firstborn enrolled in heaven, to the spirits of the righteous made perfect, and to God, the judge of all, and Jesus, the mediator of a new covenant (12.22–24). Here both creatures and Creator inhabit the heavenly world to which believers have access in the present. This access to heaven through Christ as high priest is part of their enjoyment of the good things that have come (9.11), their experience ahead of time of the salvation of 'the world to come' (2.5), of the powers of the age to come (6.4). The patriarchs looked for a promised inheritance, God's city (11.8–10). They were seeking a heavenly country, the city God had prepared (11.13–16), yet they did not receive what was promised and Christian believers are in a better position, because they already have access to this heavenly Jerusalem (cf. 11.39, 40; 12.22). At the same time believers do not yet have their full share of the promised inheritance (cf. 2.8b; 9.15; 10.34, 35). They too 'are looking for the city that is to come' (13.14).

This eschatological pattern of an experience of salvation in the present, with a focus on heaven, to be followed by the consummation of salvation at the end is exemplified in Hebrews' treatment of the concept of rest in 3.7–4.13. This takes its lead from the citation of Ps. 95.7–11, which recalls that the Israelites about to enter the promised land were refused entry to God's rest because of their rebellion. The term for 'rest' could denote either a state of rest or a resting place. In LXX Ps. 94.11 the primary meaning from the context is a local one, indicating God's resting place in the land of Canaan but also having possible associations with the sanctuary as God's resting place. But by the time Hebrews takes up this citation, the notion of God's resting place had undergone further development and had been given an eschatological interpretation in which it was associated with the heavenly Jerusalem and heavenly sanctuary. Hebrews gives the notion of rest an even broader eschatological interpretation through linking Ps. 95.11 with Gen. 2.2 (cf. 4.3, 4). The heavenly resting place awaiting the people of God is now treated as part of God's sabbath rest, which is viewed as the consummation of the divine purposes for the creation. The creation rest that God intended for humanity to share is still available. Joshua's entry into Canaan was only a type of this divine rest (cf. 4.7–9), which has been with God in heaven since the foundation of the world. In the same way that the heavenly city to which Abraham looked forward (11.10) is still to come (13.14) and yet believers already have access to it (12.22), the heavenly rest is both still to be realized and yet already accessible. Those who believe are in the process of entering the rest (4.3) but at the same time, in the tension Hebrews shares with other strands of early Christian eschatology, the consummation of the rest remains future and believers can be exhorted to 'make every effort to enter that rest' (4.11).

The relation of the horizontal and vertical dualisms in Hebrews is also raised by the way the terminology of 'to come' is employed in comparison with that of 'heavenly'. The former is used with reference to the world to come (2.5), the powers of the age to come (6.5), good things to come (10.1, cf. also 9.11) and the city to come (13.14). The latter is employed to refer to a heavenly call (3.1), the heavenly gift (6.4), the heavenly sanctuary (8.5), the heavenly things (9.23), a heavenly country (11.16) and the heavenly Jerusalem (12.22). The heavenly Jerusalem is also the city to come, as has been noted, but there is also a parallel between the heavenly gift and the powers of the age to come, since believers have already tasted both (cf. 6.4, 5). There is a further looser correlation between the heavenly things and the things to come, and between the heavenly country and the world to come. Again, therefore, it becomes clear that what is at present heavenly is also what is to come. More generally in Hebrews, the emphasis on heaven is in the sections of theological exposition, especially 8.1–10.18, while the emphasis on the future comes in the exhortation sections. Since the exposition serves the paraenesis, the vertical dualism can also be said to serve the temporal. In each case the former lays stress on what has already been achieved in Christ, while the latter sees the consummation of that salvation as still future. As a consequence, Hebrews' message is that what believers already have through partaking in Christ (and this is at present secured with him in heaven), they need to hold on to as they persevere in history and endure to the end.

Hebrews develops in two main ways the treatment of heaven and earth that it has in common with the eschatology of Jewish apocalypses and of early Christianity. The first is its stress on heaven as the realm of the permanent and eternal, in contrast to earth as the realm of the changing and transient. The second is its associated depiction of earthly phenomena as copies or shadows of heavenly ones. Again these emphases are primarily means of expressing the significance of Christ's work in its decisive, once-for-all and lasting quality. His sacrifice partakes of the quality of the end-times (9.26), the salvation he achieves is eternal (5.9; 9.12, 14; 13.20; cf. also 7.25), his priesthood is for ever (6.20; 7.17, 21, 24, 28) and his offering is for all time (10.12, 14). Christ's entry into heaven with his own blood and his session in heaven at God's right hand underline the permanent qualities of his achievement. In this light the tabernacle regulations, the sacrificial arrangements and the Levitical priesthood have to be seen as provisional, changing and transient, that is, as having the qualities that belong to the earthly. Their validity was only anticipatory. They served, in other words, as copies, sketches, symbols, shadows of the true permanent heavenly order (8.5; 9.9, 23, 24; 10.1).

Hebrews does not set out in any detail its expectations about the future. There are aspects of Christian eschatological belief that the writer has as his presuppositions and so does not need to spell out, just as he also mentions, but does not develop, the role of the Spirit or sacramental practices. There will be a final judgement (4.12; 6.2; 9.27; 10.27–31). But it is not clear how the consummation that follows such a judgement is conceived. In regard to 'the city that is to come', the English phrase 'that is to come' might suggest a coming from one place to another, but in fact the Greek participle (*mellousan*) has a purely future reference. One is therefore left to ask the question raised earlier. Does Hebrews share the early Christian perspective that is explicit elsewhere, notably in Revelation, in which a heavenly Jerusalem comes down to earth so that the life of heaven transforms that of earth, resulting in a new heaven and earth, a new creation (cf. Rev. 21.1–8); or does it conceive the future of salvation as existing in some purely heavenly eternal realm? Readers are left to fill in the gaps. How they are to do so remains disputed, but there are enough clues that may tell against the view that in Hebrews the consummation of salvation is an immaterial heavenly phenomenon.

(i) Hebrews shares the mainstream Jewish eschatological belief in the resurrection of the dead, which it mentions in passing (6.2; 11.19, 35). It would appear then that, when it lists among the inhabitants of the heavenly Jerusalem at present 'the spirits of the righteous made perfect' (12.23), these still await a future resurrection of their bodies, and the notion of bodily resurrection would have suggested a transformed spatial as well as temporal realm.

(ii) The Christological emphases of the document, particularly their incarnational aspects, reinforce this observation. The Son shared flesh and blood, became like his brothers and sisters in every respect (2.14, 17; 4.15), suffered and died (2.9, 10, 18; 5.7, 8). As high priest, he does not leave this creaturely humanity behind. The resurrection of Jesus himself is mentioned only once – in the benediction (13.20) – but it is mentioned and in a way that suggests also the resurrection of believers, since Jesus was brought back from the dead as the great shepherd of the sheep who will follow him in their own resurrection. So Jesus is exalted to heaven via the resurrection of his body from the dead. If the perfecting of Christ did not entail a mere release of the soul from the body and a purely spiritual return to the invisible world of eternal reality, then eschatological salvation for Hebrews also does not.

(iii) Elsewhere in the New Testament the coming of heaven to earth in such a way as to produce a transformed cosmos is linked with the future coming of Christ (cf. e.g. 1 Thess. 1.10; 4.14–17; Phil. 3.20, 21; Matt. 24.29–31; 25.31–46; Rev. 22.1–7, 20). Hebrews too emphasizes a second coming of Christ. The one who appeared 'at the end of the ages' to remove sin once for all will appear a second time to complete the salvation of those who eagerly await him (9.26–28). That day is approaching (10.25), and in connection with believers' full reception of what God has promised, it is asserted that 'the one who is coming will come and will not delay' (10.36, 37). This is a coming from heaven that will be the realization of Christ's cosmic inheritance (cf. 1.2), the completion of salvation through the subjection to him of the world to come (cf. 2.5–8). All this suggests that Hebrews has not abandoned the major strand of Jewish and early Christian eschatology that expected not simply a spiritual heavenly salvation but one that included transformed bodies and a transformed cosmos.

But the discussion to this point could be accused of oversimplifying and of downplaying the view that sees a far more dualistic and platonic element in the eschatology of this document. In particular, the language in which the eschatology of 12.26–29 is expressed does appear to complicate this picture and to open up the possibility that Hebrews' eschatology should be interpreted differently as the basis for a later more platonic version of eschatology in the Christian tradition, in which the goal of salvation is existence in a spiritual and immaterial heaven. Some commentators (e.g. Attridge 1989, Ellingworth 1993) see in these verses the complete destruction, rather than the renewal, of the existing creation and its replacement by an immaterial eternal realm.

The matter is important enough to justify a more detailed examination of the text. At its heart is the citation and interpretation of an earlier text from the Jewish Scriptures. This scriptural text is Hag. 2.6 – 'Yet once more I will shake not only the earth but also the heaven.' The notion of an eschatological shaking was frequently employed in apocalyptic writings (cf. 2 Bar. 59.3; 4 Ezra 6.11–17; 10.25–28) but in such writings there was the expectation of a new heaven and new earth, a transformation of the cosmos, after the shaking or after a final conflagration (cf. *4 Ezra* 7.75; 10.27; *1 Enoch* 45.4). Hebrews does not mention this. Instead it says that the text 'indicates the removal of what is shaken – that is, created things – so that what cannot be shaken may remain'. The Greek term translated here as 'removal' (*metathesis*) can in some contexts mean transformation, and if this were the case here, then the force of the passage would remain in line with Jewish eschatological notions about the transformation of the creation. But, as nearly all translations agree, in this context the term must mean removal, because there are some things from the shaken created heaven and earth that remain. That observation, however, also entails that the text cannot be saying that all the created order will be annihilated and only a sphere that is not part of the created order will remain.

What then is the force of 'created things' (*pepoiēmena*)? It is here that some have found echoes of a cosmological dualism and see the term as the equivalent of another term, *ta genomena*, 'that which has come into being or been made', which appears in Platonic literature. Their next move is to point out that Plato himself (*Timaeus* 37D) distinguishes this category from the eternal and that Philo (*Post.* 19–29) uses the same verb as is found in Heb. 12.26–28 – 'to shake' – to speak of the mutability of the earthly sphere or the created order in a cosmology where only God and the intelligible world remain unshakeable or immutable. From there it is only one further step to claim that the writer of Hebrews has read Hag. 2.6 with similar assumptions. 'For him, that which is shakeable belongs to the world of sense perceptions; and that which is perceptible to the senses is by nature transitory. . . . he knows two worlds already possessing full reality, one of which is material, and therefore, shakeable; the other is not material, and is unshakeable' (Thompson 1982: 50). On this view, that which remains is the presently invisible heavenly world, a sphere unaffected by the end-time catastrophe. The main problem with such a reading, however, is that it tends to base its reconstruction of Hebrews' eschatology and cosmology and therefore the writer's whole worldview on a few similarities in vocabulary. It does not do enough justice to the axiom that words take on a particular force from their most immediate context, so that the vocabulary employed here should primarily be interpreted within the other major assumptions that are clearly operative in Hebrews.

It has already been noted above that the text cannot be saying that all the created order will be annihilated and only a sphere that is not part of the created order will remain. Not only would that not make sense of the wording but it would also be in conflict with central aspects of Hebrews' message. Christ shares created human existence and has entered with it into the heavenly sphere and yet he remains for ever, and the thrust of the exhortation, of which 12.26–28 is a part, is that the human creatures who are readers of Hebrews should persevere in order to be part of the final unshakeable kingdom.

Two further observations about the language of this text are worth making. A number of English translations, including NRSV, are somewhat misleading in their rendering of part of v. 27 by 'the removal of what is shaken – that is, created things'. The original does not have 'that is' but a comparative particle (*hōs*) that can also function elliptically. A more literal translation is therefore not as specific and would be 'the removal of what is shaken, as of created things' or 'the removal of what is shaken, as created things are shaken', making it clearer that this is not a simple assertion that all creation will be removed.

The second point involves recalling the multivalent force of the term 'heaven' in Hebrews. Presumably, not only the visible but also the invisible heaven, with its human and angelic inhabitants (cf. 12.22–24), is envisaged as being shaken, just as elsewhere 'the heavenly things' can be said to be in need of purging through Christ's sacrifice (9.23). All creation, including the heavenly realm, is therefore capable of being shaken in a final judgement, but those created things that have been purified must be part of what remains and take their place in the unshakeable kingdom. This interpretation would be in line with the way the phrases 'not made with hands' and 'not of this creation' are employed in 9.11. Their opposites, 'made with hands' and 'of this creation' (9.24), are viewed negatively, not because they refer to the material rather than the spiritual but because they refer to what is merely created, what is subjected to transience, decay and death. Yet there is a creation that is permanent, immortal and eternal, and that is because it has been redeemed and perfected. At present it is in heaven, where Christ has been exalted, and is therefore invisible, and that is why the heavenly realm can be the focus for readers' attention in Hebrews. Such a perspective is not essentially different from that of Paul or John or Revelation. The sprinkling of vocabulary that has some similarities with that of middle Platonism simply adds to this the emphasis on permanence. Given that there will be a coming of Christ, that there will be resurrection and that the cosmos is Christ's inheritance, as is evident elsewhere in Hebrews, there is no reason to think that the unshakeable kingdom that remains will be incompatible with the redeemed and transformed materiality of bodies and cosmos.

It perhaps should not need to be stated, but this reading is not driven by any conscious concern to preserve a so-called 'pure' Jewish eschatology from contamination by 'foreign' elements. Instead, it attempts to set the passage within other major strands of Hebrews' thought. It might, of course, still be the case that the writer has incorporated into his message elements of a worldview that are in tension with other parts of that message and has not noticed the incoherence. That does not, however, appear to be the most likely option in interpreting a thinker as profound as this writer. The more plausible explanation of his use of the formulations found here is that they serve a particular emphasis, not that they introduce a type of cosmological dualism that is in conflict with his other major presuppositions. The writer develops the notion of the heavenly realm as a permanent one because he wants to depict previous revelation as provisional and the sacrificial system as based on transient phenomena in contrast to the final and unchanging revelation that has taken place in Christ.

This emphasis relates also to the unsettled, transient, impermanent factors in the readers' situation, to which attention has been drawn previously. An emphasis on the heavenly dimension within Hebrews' spatial dualism, then, is a way of making clear the realized element of the eschatological drama that is so important for the writer's pastoral exhortation. It underscores the finished work of Christ, the resulting permanent benefits for believers and the dangers of rejecting what has been accomplished. For Hebrews the regulations associated with the earthly tabernacle were symbolic of 'the present time', which carries some of the negative connotations of 'this present age' in Jewish eschatological thought (9.9). They were in place only until the 'time of correction', that of the new age and its order (9.10). Christ's permanent achievement in establishing the new order is seen in terms of his exaltation to and location in heaven as high priest, and so the 'already' of salvation is associated with heaven in its connotation of the uncreated realm of God. But that does not entail that this heaven is completely separated from humans and the temporal-spatial world that they inhabit. If their heavenly high priest completely identified himself with their humanity and if believers have links to heaven in the present, then the consummation of their salvation will fully embrace their created existence and its environment. That which lasts for ever and is at present realized primarily in heaven is the salvation of God's kingdom or rule (12.28), which includes the subjection of all things to Christ (2.8) as he inherits the cosmos created through him (1.2).

Christian existence

Through a midrashic exposition of Ps. 110.1, 4 Hebrews exhorts a community of primarily Jewish Christians to draw near to God with confidence and to persevere in hope, because Christ's heavenly high priesthood is the new covenant promise, guaranteed by oath, of the world to come. This one-sentence summary of the overall thrust of Hebrews incorporates its major themes and highlights its exhortation to a particular way of life. In it Christian existence is summarized in two main ways – drawing near to God with confidence, and persevering in hope. These are intimately linked to the two poles of the eschatological framework discussed above. The summarizing statement talks of Christ's heavenly high priesthood – the vertical pole – and the promise of the world to come – the horizontal pole. The former expresses what has already been achieved by Christ, which also functions as a guarantee of the latter, its future aspect – the fulfilment of the promise of the world's salvation. Drawing near to God relates to the vertical pole: it is the upward movement of worship. Persevering in hope relates to the horizontal pole: it is the forward movement of pilgrimage. So one way of formulating Christian existence as portrayed in Hebrews is to depict it in terms of the life of a worshipping community on the move. It is already in a relationship with God and heaven through Christ, but needs to progress towards its future salvation. It is possible to organize much of the data about Christian existence in Hebrews around these two communal movements.

Worship and cult

Hebrews pays little attention to formal aspects of the Christian cult. Baptism is mentioned; the Lord's Supper is not. Perhaps the silence about the latter is because of the preoccupation of some hearers with Jewish meals and food regulations and because, in response, the author wanted to emphasize the direct benefits of Christ's death, not their mediation through a meal. His references to the confession (3.1; 4.14; 10.23) and use of confessional formulations presuppose that these constitute part of the cultic life. But the dominant focus of Hebrews is instead on what is most essential to the movement upwards in worship. This should not be surprising since, as indicated at the beginning of this chapter, the symbolic world of Leviticus, which forms the backdrop for much of Hebrews' argument, already focuses especially on worship as the heart of God's relationship with Israel and as affecting the whole of life, and therefore lays stress on access to the presence of the holy God being properly managed.

For Hebrews too, it is paramount for the rest of Christian living in the world that this matter of access to God be properly appreciated and appropriated. As has been seen in the discussion of the work of Christ in salvation, Hebrews stresses in a variety of ways that it is Christ's sacrificial death that is the decisive factor in any authentic transition from the sphere of the unholy to that of the holy. In this connection the language of 'drawing near' or 'approaching' in worship is employed frequently (cf. 4.16; 7.19, 25; 10.1, 22; 11.6; 12.18, 22). Believers can have direct access to God, the throne of grace or the heavenly city, because Christ's death has dealt with impurity once for all and enabled them to experience forgiveness and cleansing (8.12; 9.14, 22; 10.17, 18, 22). Christ's entry as high priest into the heavenly sanctuary is not an act for himself alone but constitutes an invitation for believers to do the same. They can now offer acceptable worship, thanksgiving and praise (9.14; 12.28; 13.15). What is more, there need be no lingering sense of guilt, producing a hesitant, half-hearted approach to God, but believers are to worship with the boldness and confidence that manifest themselves in an internal assurance before God, and an external expression of honest prayer and clear and articulate confession and praise (4.16; 10.19).

Endurance and pilgrimage

The movement forwards in history towards the consummation of salvation (cf. 6.1 – 'let us go on towards perfection') will be, as has been underlined earlier in the chapter on Occasion and Purposes, in the midst of trials, marginalization, suffering and death. For this reason Hebrews consistently characterizes it in terms of the need for endurance (*hupomonē*). The Greek term can also be translated as 'patience', but this is no passive quality and is instead closely associated with the notion of persevering, the active striving to remain true to the initial confession in the face of considerable obstacles and over the long haul between the giving of the divine promise and its fulfilment (cf. 6.12, 15; 10.32, 36; 12, 2, 3, 7).

Also closely associated with endurance is faith (cf. 6.12; 10.36–39). On the one hand, faith is the essential initial and continuing underlying attitude of receptivity to and appropriation of the Christian gospel. Unlike Paul and John, Hebrews does not explicitly speak of faith in Christ. It does, however, speak of faith in God (6.1; 11.6) and in this sense the stance of faith is also closely linked to the upward movement in Christian existence, as it entails perceiving the realities of the unseen heavenly world (cf. 11.1, 2). Yet there is clearly an implicit Christological dimension to faith, since it is a response to God's initiative in Christ and to the benefits Christ bestows (cf. 3.12, 14, 19; 4.2, 3) because Christ can be depicted as not only the pioneer but also the perfecter of faith (12.2). On the other hand, and more characteristic of Hebrews' use of the term, faith shades over into faithfulness, a virtue operative in Christian living and representing the pattern of existence that remains steadfast to its Christian confession. Here the writer sees that believers need not only exhortations to faithfulness (cf. e.g. 3.6b, 12–14; 6.11, 12; 10.23; 10.36–39; 12.1, 7) but also models to follow. Christ's own faith or faithfulness is the supreme example (2.13, 17; 3.2, 6; 12.2) and this faith is, of course, viewed as also anticipated in the lives of the heroes and heroines of faith (11.4–40) and in those of the leaders the addressees have known (13.7). All were prepared to endure suffering in the present because of their conviction that there would be a future reward.

The other dominant way of depicting this essential conviction in Hebrews is through the language of 'hope'. Hope is not an attenuated vague wish for something better but a confident assurance about the future based on God's faithfulness to the promise and oath God has given in Christ (cf. 3.6; 6.11, 18–20; 7.19; 10.23; 11.1). For Hebrews, only such an assured expectation about the goal of the movement forward is able to sustain the endurance necessary and enable it to be characterized by joy rather than merely a stoical gritting of the teeth.

The movement forward in history can be viewed as a race (cf. 12.1, 12, 13), but it should not be surprising that many have held that the various ways it is treated within Hebrews are best summed up in the metaphor of pilgrimage. The letter depicts those who live by faith as 'sojourners' who are on a journey to a better country, to the city God has prepared for them (11.13–16). Indeed, key elements of a phenomenology of religious pilgrimage – separation from one place, transition or journey to a sacred place, accompanied by difficulties and the threat of failure en route, and incorporation rites on arrival at the goal – have been taken up and transformed in its exhortation to Christian living (Johnsson 1978: 244–47). Believers are on their way to glory and Jesus as pioneer has blazed the trail ahead for his followers (2.10). The goal of end-time salvation, as noted earlier, can be symbolized by the resting place in the land of Canaan, also linked to God's own rest, and believers are viewed both as already in the process of entering it and, like the wilderness generation, as still needing to make every effort to enter it (3.7–4.13). The city, to which the patriarchs looked forward, is also future and yet already prepared by God and therefore existent in heaven (11.8–16). In fulfilment of the pilgrimage motif, whereby the people of God moved from Sinai through the wilderness to Zion (cf. Ps. 68), the readers can be said to have left behind Mount Sinai and drawn near to the, at present, heavenly and invisible Mount Zion (12.18–24). Again, despite the celebration of their anticipatory arrival, they are reminded that they have not finally arrived. But their perspective on the overall pilgrimage will shape their commitment and decision-making in the present – 'Let us then go to him outside the camp and bear the abuse he endured. For here we have no lasting city, but we are looking for the city to come' (13.13, 14). Knowing that the present order is not lasting and that they are on their way to the permanent city to come, to which they already have access, should enable believers to take the risks and costs involved in identifying with Jesus, who was himself marginalized and rejected by the present order.

The life of a community on the move

Both the movement upwards and the movement forwards are those of a community. The notion of fictive kinship with its familial imagery that was common within the early Christian movement is found here in

Hebrews. The writer addresses his readers as 'brothers and sisters' (3.1, 12; 10.19; 13.22) and explains that they are children of God, and therefore not only brothers and sisters to one another but siblings of Jesus (2.10–17). The community has leaders who are to be obeyed and whose lives are to be imitated (13.7, 17), but equally essential to its thriving is the regular meeting together of its members for mutual exhortation (10.25). Only in this way will the practical solidarity that should characterize the community be nurtured (cf. 10.33, 34; 13.3).

What also becomes clear, however, is that, while it is on the way to its goal, this community is a mixed one, in which it is possible that some of its members may not in fact reach the final goal of the journey; hence the exhortations to endure and the warnings against apostasy. Whether one has genuine faith and is an authentic brother or sister of Jesus will prove itself through perseverance. Hebrews' eschatological framework is important here. Only at the end of the journey will it become clear which members of the community have been authentic in their commitment to the Christian confession. In the present there is therefore a tension, and Hebrews emphasizes both sides of it. In 2.5–3.6 the dominant tone is one of assurance and confidence because of the inseparable relationship between Jesus and his brothers and sisters, while in the following passage, 3.7–4.13, the mood shifts to one of fear lest there be exclusion from the consummation of salvation through disobedience. In fact 3.6b, which acts as a bridge between the two passages, highlights both elements. Believers constitute God's house and belong to God's people, but this is only the case if they 'hold firm the confidence and the pride that belong to hope'. In regard to the severe warnings against apostasy (cf. 6.4–8; 10.26–31; 12.15–17), interpreters have frequently either minimized their force by holding that they are treating only a hypothetical case or, like Tertullian (*Pud.* 20), exaggerated their force by stating that they allow for no repentance or forgiveness for any post-baptismal sins. The solemnity of these warnings derives from the writer's perspective on the finality and once-for-all nature of Christ's sacrifice. As Attridge (1989: 169) says of Christ's sacrifice, 'Those who reject this necessary presupposition of repentance simply, and virtually by definition, cannot repent.'

While they are on the journey, the community's members will be those who by right reasoning are trained to distinguish good from evil (5.13, 14). Their lives will be characterized not only by faith or faithfulness and hope, but also by love and good deeds (6.10; 10.24; 13.1). They will be free from the love of money or possessions (10.34; 13.5), practise hospitality (13.2), honour marriage (13.4), and, despite the treatment they may receive from others in society, will seek peace with all (12.14).

Both the community's movement upwards and its movement forwards have a Christological dimension. For the former, the major problem to be overcome is sin and a guilty conscience: the solution lies in cleansing and confident access to God, and this is supplied through Christ as high priest. For the latter, the main obstacle is disobedience and falling away: the solution is endurance in hope, and the enabling model is Christ as pioneer (2.10; 12.2).

Contrasting paradigms

The stark alternatives for living faced by the addressees are also strikingly modelled in two cameo appearances of Scriptural figures. Esau provides a negative example or warning (12.15–17). In trading his birthright for a meal, he exchanged the long-term benefits of status and security for immediate and temporary satisfaction and is judged as immoral and unholy, lacking the holiness without which no one will see God (cf. 12.14). Some of the hearers of this sermon are in danger of becoming defiled by relinquishing their inheritance of the promises as firstborn (cf. 1.14; 6.12, 17; 9.15; 12.23) in order to alleviate temporarily their physical and social hardships. It may be no accident that the term used for Esau's meal or food is a cognate of the term used for the Jewish foods or meals referred to in 9.10 and 13.9 which, as discussed in Chapter 5, appear to have remained an attraction for some of the audience. In returning to a preoccupation with such matters, they would be following Esau in finding a transient rather than permanent resolution to their problems. What is more, just as Esau later regretted bitterly his rejection of the birthright but was given no opportunity to repent, so too they might find there was no chance to be restored to repentance (cf. 6.4; 10.26–29).

On the positive side, among the Scriptural heroes listed in Hebrews 11, Moses stands out for the way in which his depiction in 11.24–27 is so explicitly adapted to speak to the situation of the readers. He refused the worldly honour and security he could have claimed as the son of Pharaoh's daughter. Instead of transient pleasures and treasures he chose marginalization in solidarity with the ill-treated people of God, thereby suffering abuse and shaming for Christ, while being unafraid of the Egyptian Pharaoh's hostility and persecution. Not only is his choice of a way of living exemplary for the hearers of Hebrews, but so also are the convictions that sustained him in it. Unlike Esau, he kept his eyes fixed on God's long-term reward (cf. 10.35; 11.6; 13.14), he persevered as if seeing 'him who is invisible' (cf. 11.1) and he believed in the efficacy of the sprinkling of blood for salvation (cf. 9.14; 12.24). In all these ways Moses remains a paradigm for the Jewish addressees of Hebrews, a paradigm of Christian existence in faith and endurance.

Further reading

On some of the theological presuppositions from the Jewish Scriptures that inform the writer, see W. Brueggemann, *Theology of the Old Testament* (Minneapolis: Augsburg Fortress, 1997), pp. 192–93; 288–93; 650–79.

For overall discussions of the major theological themes of Hebrews, see Lindars 1991; Isaacs 1992; and I. H. Marshall, *New Testament Theology* (Downers Grove, IL: InterVarsity, 2004), pp. 605–27; 682–90.

On eschatology, see the contrasting views of C. K. Barrett, 'The Eschatology of the Epistle to the Hebrews', in W. D. Davies and D. Daube (eds), *The Background of the New Testament and Its Eschatology* (Cambridge: CUP, 1956), pp. 363–93 and Thompson 1982: 41–52.

On various aspects of Christian existence in Hebrews, see W. G. Johnsson, 'The Pilgrimage Motif in the Book of Hebrews', *JBL* 97 (1978), pp. 239–51; M. N. A. Bockmuehl, 'The Church in Hebrews', in M. N. A. Bockmuehl and M. B. Thompson (eds), *A Vision for the Church: Studies in Early Christian Ecclesiology in Honour of J. P. M. Sweet* (Edinburgh: T. and T. Clark, 1997), pp. 133–51; and the monographs of Peterson 1982, Croy 1998, and Rhee 2001.

8

Some Reflections on Hebrews' Continuing Significance

The bulk of this Guide has been descriptive in its presentation of the setting, background, argument, purposes and overall thought of Hebrews. These issues are interesting in their own right. But Hebrews has remained of continuing interest for most students because it has been preserved as a foundational document of the Christian church, and the first chapter of this book touched on matters relating to its reception and continuing use by the church. For many, therefore, one of the primary reasons for wishing to find out more about Hebrews is either the conviction or the hope that the message of this document transcends its original setting and remains of significance for the thought and life of contemporary Christians. How Hebrews might do so raises major hermeneutical and theological questions that cannot be pursued at length here. Instead this final chapter will first propose that the way in which the writer of Hebrews works is itself suggestive for the theological task.

In carrying out their own theological reflection on Hebrews, readers are likely to find that there are some aspects of the epistle's analysis of and address to the human plight that are more readily appropriated because, despite the differences in time and in culture, basic human needs and Christian experience remain very much the same. One thinks, for example, of Hebrews' discussion of the bondage produced by the fear of death (cf. 2.14–18) and of the various forms of addictive behaviour in a present-day culture of death, to which its message of hope in the face of death might be applied. The pilgrimage metaphor for Christian existence also remains fruitful, as Bunyan's *Pilgrim's Progress*, with its dependence on Hebrews, illustrates for previous generations. In the midst of present-day enthusiasms for literal pilgrimages to sacred places, its implications repay further consideration as they are related to a theology of space. Another example might be Hebrews' use of heroes and heroines of faith with their subversion of the cultural values of honour and shame, which could be explored in relation to the contemporary cult of celebrity, the need for models of excellence and a theology of the virtues.

Other aspects of Hebrews' thought, however, may prove more difficult to negotiate in a theological reading of this document. Two major topics have been especially to the fore in recent discussion – its treatment of sacrifice and its attitude to Judaism – and so the rest of the chapter will offer some brief explorations of these particular issues.

Hebrews and theology

The conclusion of the earlier chapter on Genre and Rhetoric highlighted some of the merits of Hebrews as a sermon. At this point it is also worth reflecting on Hebrews as a piece of theologizing that is suggestive for the present-day task. Clearly the writer of Hebrews is a forerunner of those theologians who treat Scripture as foundational to the theological enterprise and who in fact do their theology through the reading of Scripture. His Scripture is obviously different from that of later Christian theologians. He had the Jewish Scriptures in their Greek translation. But he also had early Christian traditions about Christ in the light of which he reflected on his Scripture, and his reflections eventually became part of Christian Scripture. In embryonic form the writer of Hebrews was engaged in one of the same major tasks that confront theologians who wish to use the Bible, namely, attempting to do justice to both God's prior revelation in the Jewish Scriptures and God's new revelation in Christ.

His is not, however, the sort of Biblical theology that is content to attempt to provide some descriptive account or explanation of the two sets of revelatory data. He selects certain passages or themes to work with because he has a contemporary concern arising from the pressing needs of a specific situation in a particular Christian community. His addressees need to see that his message to them is in line with their Scriptures read in the light of the Christian confession, and that such a reading calls them to continued faith and to appropriate worship and behaviour in their distinctive setting.

There is a two-fold dialectic at work in the theology of Hebrews. First, the significance of what has happened in Christ interprets prior revelation, but that prior revelation also interprets what has happened in Christ. Second, Scripture read through the lenses of the Christian confession sheds light on and shapes the present situation of writer and readers, but that present situation also sheds light on and shapes how Scripture is read through the lenses of the Christian confession. Both dialectics mean that this theological reading of Scripture calls for discernment. Discernment needs to be exercised in seeing what remains constant in God's previous revelation and what has changed because of the further decisive revelation in Christ, and in seeing how a combination of these factors is related to particular sets of circumstances of Christian believers in the world. For the writer of Hebrews this entailed critical discernment, as he wrestled with the questions of where the continuity between the two stages of revelation lies, and where the discontinuity between them is such that parts of the former have to be critiqued and pronounced no longer directly applicable. Other essential ingredients in his theological discernment and its articulation include imagination and creativity wedded to a mastery of contemporary exegetical and rhetorical skills.

His combination of theological reflection and ethical exhortation is also highly instructive. It reflects the way in which his thinking is shaped by and feeds into pastoral concerns. There is a sense in which, like Hebrews, all good theology is applied theology, rooted in and finding coherent connections within the Christian tradition, but also articulated in such a way as to be pertinent to the thoughts and issues of its own time and place. Again Hebrews shows how its writer's understanding of the significance of what God has accomplished in Christ not only challenges, but also is inevitably shaped by, the worldview of his day. This is indicated, for example, by the way in which the cultural values of honour and shame permeate his thought. It is also seen in his overall worldview, where, as has been noted, he is primarily informed by the Jewish eschatology found in apocalyptic writings. But he is also apparently a Hellenistic Jew who has been influenced by some of the thinking and formulations of the middle Platonism of his time, so that he can talk of the contrast between earthly shadows and their true form in the heavenly invisible world, and of that between the transient world and a more permanent and stable realm. If, then, Hebrews is suggestive for contemporary theology, the latter will be the sort of theology that interprets the whole of Scripture in the light of Christian beliefs informed by the theological tradition, by contemporary thought, and by the perceived needs of the church in its role in the world.

For Hebrews, 'Jesus Christ is the same yesterday and today and for ever' (13.8). The witness to his identity and significance, however, is made in the particular contexts of yesterday or today. If he is to be appreciated as the mediator who is able to sympathize with human weaknesses and to provide grace for human needs, then it will not be sufficient simply to repeat or rehearse the language of Hebrews or of yesterday's interpreters. What is needed is to learn from them in thinking through the implications of the Christian gospel for analysing and exposing the needs of the present time. It should be no surprise that for the most part the theologizing of Hebrews takes the form of a sermon, since the best preaching involves precisely the sort of theological reflection that endeavours to hear the word of God afresh for a new setting. Theology, on this view, is not merely an academic luxury or a hobby for those with a particular bent. It is not an activity that can be jettisoned by the busy preacher in favour of providing some inspirational advice for the real business of getting on with the practical aspects of life. Rather, theology is for the sermon because theology is essential for Christian living. Unless they are related to coherent convictions about the gospel, God and the world, activities including organizational strategies, working for justice and serving the disadvantaged are likely soon to run out of energy. The writer of Hebrews had already perceived that a lack of mature theological reflection, and a tendency to drift, go hand in hand (cf. 5.11–6.12).

But theology that takes Hebrews as one possible model for its task will also need to consider whether, if Hebrews can critique and relativize parts of its authoritative Scripture in the light of what is perceived to have happened in Christ, it too should be prepared to critique and relativize parts of its Scriptures – including now, of course, the New Testament – in the light of its central confession about Christ. To do so would not imply the possession of some further normative revelation but rather entail that the same norm employed by Hebrews is applied to the documents that are the human, and therefore culturally conditioned, witnesses to the eschatological fulfilment in Christ, and that are not simply to be identified with that fulfilment. It is relatively straightforward, but still by no means undisputed, to see what this might mean for places in which the New Testament writers' application of the gospel is shaped by the patriarchy or the views of sexuality of their time. It calls for even greater discernment to see the implications for areas much more central to early Christian proclamation, such as the use of sacrificial imagery for depicting the significance of Christ's death or notions of supersession in relation to Judaism. The dominance of these two matters in Hebrews is such that its interpreters cannot avoid some reflection on them.

Sacrifice and the death of Christ

The centrality of Hebrews' depiction of the death of Christ as sacrifice has been seen in the section on Salvation in the previous chapter, and some of the hermeneutical issues surrounding this depiction will have already been suggested by the attempt to set out at the beginning of that chapter the presuppositions Hebrews inherits from the Jewish Scriptures and cultic practices about holiness and atonement. The questions here are whether Hebrews' interpretation of the saving significance of Christ's death, which is informed by such presuppositions, should any longer play a part in contemporary Christian theology, and whether its dominant sacrificial metaphor should now be treated as a dead one that needs to be replaced by different understandings of salvation.

The abandonment of the sacrificial metaphor is frequently advocated and for a variety of reasons. Some writers simply take for granted that the literal practices of bloody animal sacrifices on which it is dependent are relics of a primitive past that can have no significance in the contemporary world. Others point to what they see as its limitations or to the dysfunctional effects of its traditional or popular interpretations, and consider it not worthy of retrieval. Among the list of objections raised are the following.

- To insist on the necessity of sacrifice presupposes not a merciful, compassionate God but a God too concerned about affronts to the divine character and status.
- The notion that God is somehow to be placated by a ritual involving blood is superstitious and magical.
- The view that a priest can offer a vicarious sacrifice on behalf of others offends against modern convictions about individual autonomy and moral responsibility.
- In the case of Christ, the sacrifice metaphor involves God as Father willing the death of the Son in a form of 'divine child abuse'.
- It underwrites the notion that suffering is itself a virtue and this has had disastrous consequences in the Christian tradition, especially for the lives of women.

If what is objected to in much of this catalogue were really entailed by Hebrews' presentation of Christ's death as a sacrifice, then it would certainly be time for the radical conclusion that the metaphor can no longer be used responsibly and that this central feature of Hebrews' message is now only of interest to historians of early Christianity. When subjected to analysis, however, some of the objections can be seen to come from assumptions that are in any case alien to what would normally be taken to be Christian theology. Others derive from a lack of appreciation of the meaning of sacrifice and the extent to which its symbolism reflects universal human values and remains relevant. Other objections still result from an inadequate grasp, which sometimes becomes caricature, of how Hebrews (and indeed other parts of the New Testament) actually presents the death of Christ as sacrifice and links it to other parts of its message.

Space does not permit adequate explication or justification here, but this discussion takes it for granted that Christian theology operates with the conviction of the reality of a transcendent holy and loving triune God and of this God's good creation which has become alienated, disordered and polluted through humanity's inappropriate response to its Creator. The first part of this conviction rules out the misunderstanding that, in order to deal with sin, God imposes a violent death on an unwilling Son.

Indeed, Hebrews' presentation makes it clear that the pre-existent Son as part of the triune God comes into the world and takes on full humanity in order to experience death on behalf of humanity and to offer himself voluntarily as a sacrifice (cf. 1.2, 3; 2.9, 10, 17; 10.5–10). Jesus is depicted not only as the sacrifice but also as the priest who offers the sacrifice. What is more, all three persons of the trinity are involved – 'how much more will the blood of Christ, who through the eternal Spirit offered himself without blemish to God, purify our conscience from dead works to worship the living God!' (9.14). Through the death of the incarnate Son the triune God graciously provides a solution to humanity's plight. There is no sense in which Christ's death as sacrifice is to be seen either as the attempt of the Son to placate or change the mind of a Father who is unwilling to be merciful, or as the imposition of a cruel death by a tyrannical Father on an unwilling Son.

The second part of the basic Christian conviction rules out inappropriate notions of individual human autonomy that allow no room for representative or vicarious solutions to the human plight. Along with Scripture as a whole, Hebrews has a conceptual world in which blame for the human plight cannot simply be parcelled out precisely to individuals, because humans have unleashed an alienation and disorder that goes beyond the individual, involves others in its taint, has a collective and corporate dimension, and extends even to the non-human creation. If humans were morally isolated individuals, if they were not caught up in histories of oppression and victimization, and if there were no pervasive and systemic evil, then, to be sure, it would make no sense to think of a connection between the life of Jesus and the lives of other humans or to consider his death as a vicarious sacrifice. Hebrews, however, stresses the solidarity between Jesus as the incarnate Son and other humans that counteracts the solidarity of humans in slavery to sin and the fear of death, and enables him as humanity's representative to bring about a new situation that no other human acting as an autonomous moral agent could accomplish (cf. esp. 2.10–18).

This divine initiative in dealing with human impurity and restoring holiness was already anticipated in the Jewish sacrificial system. The discussion in the previous chapter already warned against simply dismissing the assumptions that made sense of such sacrifices as primitive and pointed to present-day concerns about pollution and disorder in society and the environment. But it is worth recalling that sacrificial rituals were not limited to Judaism but have been a part of a variety of religions and cultures. No one general theory about the origins and functions of sacrifice has commanded assent. Nevertheless, whether sacrifices are seen as functioning as gifts to gain the favour of other humans or the gods, as establishing communion through feasting on the sacrifice, as aggressively removing something (guilt or a scapegoat) from which humans wish to distance themselves, or as some combination of all three, it can be argued that they are symbolic expressions of the universal principle that life lives and is enhanced and reordered at the expense of other life (cf. Theissen 1999: 151–55). To view Jesus' death as a sacrifice, then, is to address the deep and continuing human experience of attempting to cope with and gain from the struggle for life. His death enhances and reorders human life by dealing with moral impurity and providing full access to God, and at the same time it brings an end to the need for humans to enrich their lives at the cost of other lives. Because of the death of this one victim of violence, there would be no further need either for the offering of many bloody animal sacrifices or for its underlying rationale in which other humans are viewed as obstacles to be overcome or violently removed in competition for the enhancement of life.

In this way the metaphor of sacrifice as applied to Jesus' death is dependent on sacrificial rituals and their significance but at the same time decisively transforms them. In Hebrews there is now only the unique once-for-all sacrifice of Christ, and the sacrifices that remain for believers are the giving of their own lives through the activities of verbal praise to God and displaying kindness to and communion with other humans (13.15, 16). Just as the necessity for sacrifices that destroy other life has been removed, so has the need for any self-annihilating sacrifices, such as the sort of self-abnegation that is simply willing to accept habitual physical or mental abuse without non-violent confrontation of its evil. It is not all suffering or suffering per se that is redemptive but rather the once-for-all suffering of Christ.

It should also be clear that sacrifice as applied to the death of Christ is not, as it is sometimes described, a distinctly limited and backward-looking metaphor, treating only the effects of that death in relation to the past and its sins. It takes up both the purgative and the reparative significances of Jewish sacrifices, cleansing from stain but also transformatively renewing relationship. The obvious should also not be forgotten. Unlike the victims of other sacrifice, Christ as victim does not remain dead. Hebrews links Christ's death and resurrection through its notion of his exaltation, whereby his once-for-all sacrifice is made continually available and effective through his continuing presence and intercession before God as high priest. He therefore not only provides the removal of guilt and forgiveness of sins but also a new relationship, that of the new covenant, based on the power of Christ's indestructible life and introducing a better hope (7.15–19), the hope of a restored cosmos, the world to come (2.5). Because Hebrews envisages Christ as high priest entering heaven with his definitive sacrifice, that sacrifice is not simply an event of the past but has a forward-looking significance whereby its benefits open up and maintain a relationship with God that enables humans to endure with joy on their way to the future for which they were created.

Sacrifice is a category that is central to both testaments and that facilitates Christians reading the two as a whole, finding both continuity and discontinuity in God's purposes for human flourishing, and seeing Christ as the fulfilment and enabler of those purposes. Hebrews' use of this category as a metaphor for Christ's death sheds light on the reality that God in Christ has brought about a change within history that humans left to themselves could never accomplish. By its nature this metaphor serves as a constant reminder of an essential Christian conviction about the relation of God and the world, namely, that God as the transcendent, holy and gracious Creator has taken the initiative in solving the problem of the deadly disorder of humanity's polluted and polluting condition. It indicates that the solution is concentrated in the violent death of Jesus, which, because it is the death of the incarnate Son and is followed by his exaltation, is able both to remove the taint of moral pollution and to inaugurate a reordered and enhanced life for creation. What Hebrews says about the role of Christ as mediator in the whole narrative of salvation can be said, also in retrospect, of its central image for his death – it is entirely 'fitting'. Rather than abandoning it, therefore, this way of viewing the import of Christ's death needs to be freshly appreciated and then articulated in ways that do not contribute to the distortions of its meaning that, for some, have made it seem so problematic.

Attitude to Judaism

As will already have become abundantly clear from the earlier discussions, not least the chapter on Hebrews' use of Scripture, its writer holds that, while the Scripture is still the authoritative vehicle of God's self-disclosure, the sacrificial system, the law and the Sinaitic covenant, of which Scripture speaks, have been surpassed by God's new and decisive word in Christ, and so in terms of present Christian experience are no longer appropriate. The law, its symbols and institutions remain crucial for interpreting the fulfilment of God's purposes in Christ but do not determine Christian practice. Christ's once-for-all sacrifice does away with the need for the sacrificial system (cf. 10.4–18) and indeed the covenant with Moses can be described as obsolete (8.13). It is in this sense that Hebrews can be appropriately called a 'supersessionist' document.

But does that mean that it is also anti-Jewish? This may at first sight seem a surprising question to ask about a text written by a Jewish Christian to, in all probability, other Jewish Christians. Nevertheless, it can be argued that the implications of its message lead to a perspective on Judaism that is anti-Jewish. One Jewish scholar has recently claimed that precisely such an attitude is the result of its reading of the Jewish Scriptures through Christological lenses. 'The Epistle to the Hebrews demonstrates more thoroughly than any other New Testament document the christocentric interpretation of the Jewish Bible used as evidence of the obstinacy, and therefore moral turpitude of the Jewish people' and 'when the old covenant is labelled "obsolete" (8:13) it is only a small shift to imagine the old covenant people as "obsolete" as well' (Koosed 2002: 95, 96). The same scholar goes on to argue that the antisemitism of Nazi Germany was directed at the Jew as the enemy within, and that the Other within is always more threatening than the Other outside. Because it still incorporates Judaism within its theology, Hebrews is charged with laying the very foundations for this sort of violent attitude, although it is conceded that its original writer and readers did not have the power to take violent measures against anyone (cf. Koosed 2002: 96–7, 99).

In attempting to assess such a charge, it is worth stepping back in order to clarify some related issues. One might first ask how other Jews of the time are likely to have responded to Hebrews. We have no direct evidence, but clearly the convictions expressed in the epistle would have brought those who held them into a conflict with other Jews over the outworking of the purposes of the God of Israel and over the identity of the true people of God. Non-Christian Jews exposed to such convictions could not have accepted their basic premise that what had happened in Jesus was God's decisive revelation, but would they have been offended by its assertions about the implications of that conviction? They might well have been prepared in principle to accept that Scripture could receive a new application in relation to the Messiah, but could not have tolerated the Christian claim that the crucified Jesus of Nazareth was the Messiah nor the amount of discontinuity with the law that this particular messianic claim entailed.

If Hebrews is dated after 70 CE, then fellow Jews might not have been offended by its viewing the sacrificial system as outmoded or even imperfect, since for very different reasons they also had to come to terms with the passing of this institution. But again it is likely to have been a very different matter in regard to the conclusions drawn from this about the status of the law and the covenant with Moses. Any reworking of ideas about the sacrificial system within mainstream Judaism was done within the framework of the lasting validity of the Mosaic covenant as a whole. Assertions in Hebrews, therefore, about the obsolescence of the first covenant are unlikely to have been anything other than offensive, whatever might be made by other Jews of expectations of a new covenant on the basis of prophetic passages. Talk of a 'new covenant' serves as a reminder of another group within early-first-century Judaism for whom this had been a prominent theme.

The writings of the Qumran community also interpreted Scripture in the light of a later Jewish figure, the Teacher of Righteousness, and, viewing their own community as the setting for the true form of Judaism, the Qumran community were dismissive of its other contemporary manifestations. In fact, they stopped participating in the sacrificial system, because they held the Jerusalem temple to be defiled. However, this was not, of course, a rejection of sacrificial worship in principle, since they hoped for a future restoration of a purified cult. Little is known of how some of their more extreme claims would have been received by the majority of Jews, but their very existence is one of the pieces of evidence that Hebrews could have been seen as taking its place in an ongoing conflict, often accompanied by very sharp polemic, within first-century Judaism over the appropriation and interpretation of its major symbols.

It is more important, however, to ask what sort of attitude to non-Christian Jews Hebrews would have encouraged among its own readers. As Wilson (1995: 110–11) rightly points out, this is a question to which not enough attention is paid. His own answer is that 'the author would have encouraged his readers . . . to form a clear and unambiguous judgement: Judaism is defunct, because it has been surpassed' (Wilson 1995: 122–23). But if, as is most likely, author and readers were themselves Jews, this answer requires qualification. Indeed, the notion of this document's relation to Judaism could be held to be an anachronistic one, if it suggests that author and readers saw themselves as standing outside their religious heritage and having an attitude towards its basic set of convictions from which they had now distanced themselves by converting to the new religion of Christianity. Rather, from their own perspective, it was not so much that Judaism was defunct but more that their religion and its central symbols had now been decisively fulfilled in Christ, and that because of this fulfilment new ways of expressing their worship of and obedience to Israel's God had become appropriate, and new ways of interpreting their Scriptures had become inevitable.

Nevertheless, it is also the case that these Jewish Christians were a minority and that the conflict of their beliefs with those of the majority of Jews was already entailing decisions with social consequences about whether their primary allegiance lay with the majority or with their own small assemblies of Jewish Christians. Talking of Hebrews' attitude to Judaism is in this qualified sense not anachronistic, since it reminds us that what has come to be called 'the parting(s) of the ways' is already implicit in this epistle's exhortations (cf. 13.12, 13). Yet those who depict Hebrews as engaged in hostile conflict with Judaism are wide of the mark. Rather than being anti-Jewish, its generative conviction that God has acted decisively in Jesus as Messiah to inaugurate a new order is the product of a Jewish eschatological perspective. It then conducts its critiques of the old order through reasoned interpretations of a common Scripture. In the process that old order is by no means despised, but rather seen as necessary anticipation. The discussion in 3.1–6 could not be clearer in its tone: Moses was faithful and deserving of honour, but Jesus is worthy of greater honour.

But this is still to talk of an attitude to Judaism, the mother religion and its symbols and institutions, and not to talk of any stance toward those who remained in it. On this matter Hebrews is virtually silent. It does not reflect on why others have not come to believe in Jesus, or on their destiny. It might be claimed that, since it warns of judgement for those who fail to continue in their belief, it assumes the same fate for those who have failed to believe in the first place. But this is outside its concerns, and in any case the notion of some form of judgement awaiting humans at the end was a familiar belief within Judaism itself and often used as a threat in disputes. One should perhaps assume that it was expected that the truth of its writer's and readers' own confession about Jesus would become clear to all at the rapidly approaching final Day (10.25b). In the meanwhile, however, there is certainly no excoriation of unbelieving Jews or of what Koosed calls 'the obstinacy, and therefore moral turpitude of the Jewish people'. Instead, when outsiders, both Jews and Gentiles, do come into view, the exhortation is a striking one – 'Pursue peace with everyone' (12.14).

It is one thing to show that, while Hebrews sees the Mosaic covenant and its institutions as passing away and no longer necessary because of what has happened in Christ, it does not itself take a negative stance toward other Jewish people. It is quite another matter, however, to attempt to defend some of its later influence in this way. Once the separation between the Christian movement and Judaism had clearly set in after 135 CE and Hebrews became a text whose later readers were primarily Gentile Christians who had little contact with the Judaism of their own time, then its critique of the earlier stage of Judaism as obsolete in the light of its fulfilment in Christ would easily have been thought to apply to Judaism as such. The continuing phenomenon of Judaism could then appear to be an anomaly with no authentic raison d'être and, worse, what Koosed describes as the 'small shift' from thinking of the religion as surpassed to thinking of its practitioners in a similar way could also all too easily be made. The presence of Jewish synagogues across the empire appeared to give the lie to Christian claims that Judaism had become bankrupt in the light of its fulfilment. While Paul had spoken earlier of the spiritual blindness of both the Jewish and Gentile unbelievers of his own day (cf. 2 Cor. 3.14–4.4), now the Jewish people in particular were singled out as the most heinous examples of such blindness and as especially prone to sin (cf. e.g. Tertullian, *Adv. Marc.* 2.18.2–3), and the only explanation for their continued existence was found in their dispersion and merited subjection being a sign of divine judgement for their rejection of their Messiah (cf. e.g. Augustine, *Adv. Faust. Man.* 12.12). Theological judgements about the subjection of Jews to Christians, who had replaced them as the people of God, were construed as entailing their necessary political and social subjection and easily became linked with popular antisemitism in the Greco-Roman world. 'Supersessionism' in its most damaging form had emerged in Christian thinking, writing and practice.

When 'supersessionism' is under discussion, it is frequently indicted in all its forms, but it is necessary to distinguish between the different aspects of this phenomenon. After all, there is a sense, as Gordon (2000: 27–28) suggests, in which both Christianity and Judaism are supersessionist in regard to the religion of the Jewish Scriptures. Both abandoned the central form of worship that involved approaching God by means of animal sacrifices and developed new systems for dealing with the major concerns of holiness and sin. Both developed new sets of authoritative writings through which the Jewish Scriptures were to be interpreted. But such observations take us only so far. Judaism remains in strong continuity with its Scriptures in holding the study and practice of Torah to be its covenantal worship of the one true God. What Hebrews says about the passing of the old covenant with its law and the fulfilment of the promise of a new covenant in Christ stands in clear contradiction to this. And there is surely a sense in which this sort of Christological supersessionism was inevitable for the early Christian movement and remains non-negotiable as part of Christianity's 'scandal of particularity'. Without the conviction that Christ was the surpassing fulfilment of the Mosaic covenant, there would have been no reason in the first place for Jews to have become Christians or to remain Christians under pressure (the issue for Hebrews) or for Gentiles to have become Christians rather than proselytes or God-fearers. Without the conviction that Jesus Christ is the decisive revelation of God for all human beings, however the implications of that conviction are spelled out, Christianity is no longer recognizably in continuity with its Scriptural foundation. The suggestion, sometimes made today, that Christians should think in terms of two covenants, one for Jews, based on Moses, and one for Gentiles, based on Jesus, does not allow Jesus to be the decisive revelation for the people to whom this revelation was given in the first place.

The key questions, with which much recent theology has been wrestling since the Holocaust, are whether, and if so how, this distinctive claim for Jesus can be maintained without having as its inevitable concomitant the other sort of supersessionism, in which it is held that the church has displaced the Jewish people as God's elect and the religious validity of the synagogue and its adherents is denied. There is no space to pursue these questions at any length, but Christians are surely committed to a positive answer to the first question. At least one part of the response to the second will be to keep perpetual guard lest, in the reception of documents like Hebrews, the 'small shift' from critical assessment of the Mosaic covenant to judgemental assessment of those for whom it remains foundational take place. It should now be all too plain that the theological judgement that Jews had no reason to continue to live as Jews but should become Christians fed into the evil political judgement of Nazi Germany that Jews had no reason to continue to live.

In relation to Hebrews the issue is also bound up with a significant difference between the position of present-day Christians and those of the New Testament period. The latter, including the writer of Hebrews, expected the theological tension between Christians and non-Christian Jews to be resolved within a generation by the parousia of Christ at the end of the age. While not neglecting significant elements of continuity with the Jewish past, the emphasis of Hebrews in its rhetoric and theology is to stress the 'already' of God's decisive word in Christ in such a way as to draw strong negative deductions about central elements of that past, in order to prevent its readers simply drifting back to their previous convictions. As with all powerful theological statements forged in particular and contingent settings, there are likely to be both gains and losses when these are appropriated by later generations who are removed from the original situations that produced them. This is particularly so in the case of Hebrews. Over against the gains in insight into Christology, the atonement, the nature of Christian existence and the decisive newness of the covenant established in Christ, have to be set the losses, once its later readers are primarily Gentile Christians, of any existential sense of continuity with a Jewish heritage and of their being encouraged to think of Judaism, to take up Wilson's language, simply as 'defunct, because it has been surpassed'. When the 'not yet' of Hebrews has turned into over nineteen hundred years in which both the Jewish synagogue has continued and Gentile Christian attitudes to Jews have often been lamentable and entailed tragic consequences, some different theologizing from that of Hebrews, though no less faithful and creative, may well be required (cf. also Salevao 2002: 410–12). With Hebrews, it will grapple with the consequences of an affirmation of God's once-for-all revelation in Christ, while attempting to do greater justice to the positive witness of an ongoing Judaism, to God's continuing election of the Jewish people, despite the majority's rejection of Jesus as Messiah (cf. Rom. 11.28, 29), and to the acknowledgment that 'God's history with Israel and the nations is the permanent and enduring medium of God's work as the Consummator of human creation and therefore . . . also the permanent and enduring context of the gospel about Jesus' (Soulen 1996:110).

In rethinking the appropriation of this aspect of Hebrews, there can be no easy, if well-intentioned, solutions which compromise the integrity of the Christian 'yes' and the Jewish 'no' to Jesus as the incarnation of God. There is no escaping the contradiction and dispute that this entails while living in the hope that the eschaton will provide the resolution that is not yet apparent. In the meanwhile, one thing should be clear for Christians – whether they are oppressed, as in the case of the addressees of Hebrews, or whether they are in positions of power: the 'otherness' of the Jewish other is to be genuinely respected. All violence, including that of holding that, religiously, Judaism no longer deserves to exist, is to be eschewed. On this Hebrews itself is unambiguous. Christians are to take as the model for their living the one who was willing to renounce all claims to honour and power in order to become the victim of the world's violence (13.12, 13) and, in so doing, they are actively to seek peace with all (12.14).

Further reading

On the relation of the theologizing of the writer of Hebrews to the task of theology, see further A. T. Lincoln, 'Hebrews and Biblical Theology', in C. Bartholomew et al. (eds), *Out of Egypt: Biblical Theology and Biblical Interpretation* (Carlisle: Paternoster, 2004), pp. 313–38.

For a structuralist anthropological discussion of sacrifice, see Dunnill 1992: 64–111, and for an account of the sacrificial death of Jesus as part of the early Christian sign system, see G. Theissen, *A Theory of Primitive Christian Religion* (London: SCM, 1999), pp. 139–60.

For positive assessments of the continuing value of sacrifice as a central metaphor for the atonement, see, for example, C. E. Gunton, *The Actuality of the Atonement* (Edinburgh: T and T Clark, 1988), pp. 115–41 and, more recently, R. Sherman, *King, Priest, and Prophet* (London: T and T Clark International, 2004), pp. 169–218.

On Hebrews and Judaism, see further S. G. Wilson, *Related Strangers. Jews and Christians 70–170 C.E.* (Minneapolis: Fortress, 1995), pp. 110–27; J. L. Koosed, 'Double Bind: Sacrifice in the Epistle to the Hebrews', in T. Linafelt (ed.), *A Shadow of Glory: Reading the New Testament after the Holocaust* (London: Routledge, 2002), pp. 89–101.

For attempts to deal with the continuing validity of Judaism from a Christian perspective, see, for example, R. K. Soulen, *The God of Israel and Christian Theology* (Minneapolis: Fortress, 1996) and B. Marshall, 'Christ and the Cultures: The Jewish People and Christian Theology', in C. E. Gunton (ed.), *The Cambridge Companion to Christian Doctrine* (Cambridge: CUP, 1997), pp. 81–100.

Index of References

Index of Authors